D1030198

The Military History of THE KOREAN WAR

THE MILITARY HISTORY OF THE KOREAN WAR

by S. L. A. MARSHALL

BRIGADIER GENERAL, USAR (RET.)

Operations Analyst, Eighth Army, Korea

Chief Historian, European Theater

FRANKLIN WATTS, INC.

575 Lexington Avenue • New York 22

To General Matthew B. Ridgway
who built high the faith in
fighting Americans because
they strengthened from
all they saw of him.

Library of Congress Catalog Card Number: 63-8865

Printed in the United States of America
by Polygraphic Company of America, Inc.

1 2 3 4 5 6 7

Contents

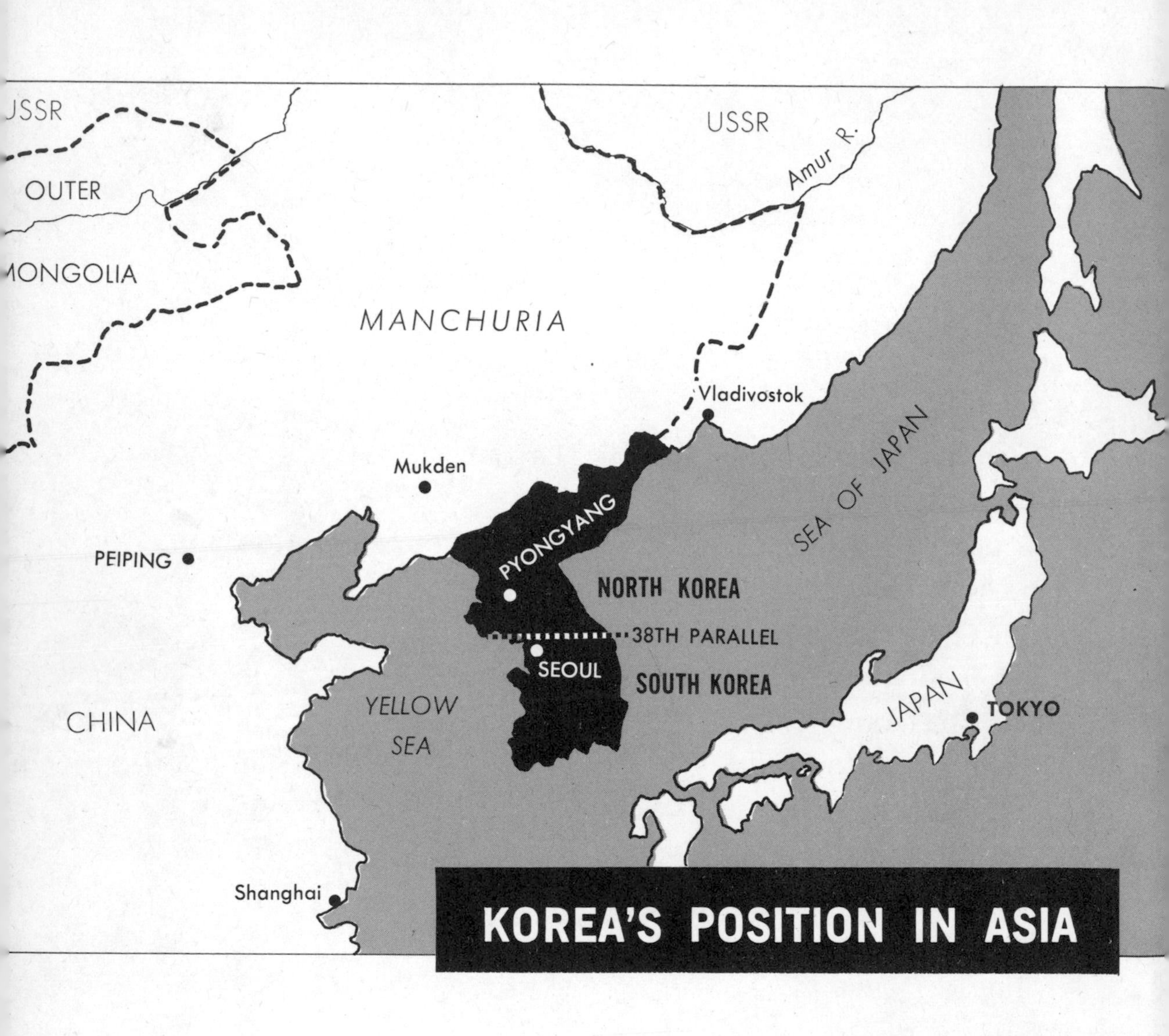
USSR
USSR
Amur R.
OUTER
MONGOLIA
MANCHURIA
Vladivostok
Mukden
SEA OF JAPAN
PYONGYANG
PEIPING
NORTH KOREA
38TH PARALLEL
SEOUL
SOUTH KOREA
JAPAN
TOKYO
YELLOW
SEA
CHINA
Shanghai
KOREA'S POSITION IN ASIA

No Small War

For many reasons the Korean War, which began in 1950 and ended with an unstable truce in 1953, is one of the most important events of the twentieth century. Looked at in perspective, it influenced the position of the United States in relation to all other nations as profoundly as either World War I or World War II. Yet, paradoxically, even Americans who know their military history almost never think of it that way. Because it did not end in total victory for the United States and its allies, most Americans either complain that it cost much and accomplished nothing, or regard it as a minor incident in their own nation's climb to world leadership.

For political reasons, official Washington does not even classify the Korean War as a war, but rather, as a "police action." The justification for such a classification is that the struggle was a collective effort by seventeen nations under the United Nations flag simply to restrain Communist aggression, rather than to punish the aggressors and deprive them of territory.

Statistics, however, tell a different story. The Korean "police action" was the costliest small war in which the military forces of the United States ever engaged. In lives sacrificed, wounds received, and Americans made prisoner by the enemy, Korea was almost as deadly for the United States as World War I. The dollar costs have never been computed, but they would range in the billions. The United States was engaged longer in Korea than in all other wars excepting the American Revolution, the Civil War, and World War II. No, it was not a minor affair.

The results of the Korean War are no less significant than its high price. Above all, it reaffirmed and at last made certain that the United States was forever done with what it called "isolationism." Before World War II, the United States had refused to ally itself with other peace-minded states. Great distances and wide oceans separated it from strong military nations which might otherwise have threatened its security. Lulled by the belief that distance kept it safe, the United States had always stayed less than half armed.

Beginning with World War I, the rise of military air power steadily diminished distance until America could no longer avoid becoming involved in the great power struggles within the Old World. By the end of World War II, the United States was remote from Europe in neither time nor space. Actually, it had come within a few hours' range of main weapons based on other continents. Today, the rise of ballistic missiles has reduced the interval to minutes.

During and after World War II the United States signed treaties of mutual aid and defense with other nations. It renounced isolationism, but it continued to act like an isolated country. For example, after World War II, just as after World War I, it rapidly demobilized its giant military machine and prepared to withdraw its garrison from occupied West Germany. Russia, on the other hand, not only kept its forces intact, but modernized them and greatly expanded its armament industry.

It took the Korean War to drive home to the United States that any number of alliances, if not supported by strong military preparedness, would never restrain aggression. In the middle of the Korean War the United States reorganized and doubled in size its Seventh Army in Europe. After the fighting in Korea ceased, the United States, for the first time, did not demobilize its armed forces. It lowered manpower levels in the Army, Navy, and Air Forces only slightly. It held together its Eighth Army, which had carried the brunt of the fighting in Korea, and kept it in Korea. It steadily improved and increased its military weapons.

These changes in American policy mark the real importance of the Korean War. The United States at last realized that the Communist powers — Russia and Red China — would not stop, that they could only *be stopped;* that their design for world conquest is not negotiable and that the one check to it is the possession of superior power.

For America, this acceptance of an ugly truth was a decided gain. The country had to be shocked into a realistic appreciation of the forces that would destroy democracy the world over. At the same time, the Korean War warned the two great Communist powers that the United States would take great risks for the sake of a principle, even though its own territory was not immediately threatened.

The Korean War was important for other reasons, too. It was the first time the United Nations had been called upon to prove that it would act as well as talk. Never had the United Nations, or its predecessor, the League of Nations, made war or taken any main risk to stop an aggressor. Yet this had to happen some time if the United Nations was to endure. The old League of Nations had failed because it did not use force to halt the aggressions of such power-greedy nations as Hitler's Germany and Mussolini's Italy. The United Nations, like the old League, had been formed primarily to settle disputes between nations. In the case of the Communist aggression in Korea, it not only denounced the act but went to war to halt it.

Korea was an old-fashioned kind of war. Its fighting was dominated far more by field artillery, machine guns, and rifles than by bombing planes, medium tanks, and aircraft carriers. These modern implements, along with paratroops, did occasionally figure in the fighting, but for the most part, the war was fought along pre-twentieth-century lines. Hand-to-hand combat was common. Bayonets and hand grenades were widely used, as were barbed wire and field mines.

That both sides were content to have it so was reassuring and significant. The United States had ended World War II by dropping atomic bombs on two Japanese cities, and Russia, which acted as arms supplier to its Communist allies and to Red China, had begun to make atomic bombs. For five years the whole world had been afraid that any small war in which either the United States or Russia took part would quickly turn into an atomic war. Korea was the first test of that dread possibility. The results proved that the atomic powers are fearful of opening Pandora's box, and that the possession of arsenals capable of obliterating the world's population has bred in governments a wholly new measure of restraint. This, too, makes the Korean War an important chapter in the story of the twentieth century.

Korea – The Country and Its History

THERE IS NO coastwise country in the world less suited than Korea to the movement of military forces in war, and there is none that offers so little comfort and reward to its conquerors.

Almost the entire length of the country is mountainous, and the ridgeline heights are massive rock. At best, only small shrubs, stunted trees, and sparse grass maintain a foothold on the eroded slopes. There are no thick forests anywhere. The few hard-surface roads that run between the larger cities never have more than two lines of pavement, and this pavement is laid so thin that it cracks everywhere. Away from the main arteries of traffic there are only dirt tracks suitable for oxcarts and pedestrians. The few bridges that span the waterways are usually crudely built, and capable of handling one-way traffic only. The usual river crossing is a ford. Most of the valley floors are so narrow that there is room only for a narrow path or a brook-size stream bed.

Wherever it is possible to till the land – along the flats, within the draws or on the lower slopes, there is usually a mud-bottomed rice paddy. These are forbidden ground to wheeled vehicles or troops with heavy guns. Arable land is so scarce and so precious that the craggy tops of the lower ridges are used for burial ground. These ridges go on and on as far as the eye can see. All fighting in Korea is either uphill or down. Coping with the hills is more exhausting to fighting forces than meeting the fire of the enemy.

Korea's population is tragically poverty-stricken because most of the land is sterile. There are few mineral resources in the mountains, and almost no timber to speak of. Wild fruit and berries are scarce. Except in the far north, the rivers are useless for industry because after the rainy season, which comes in spring and summer, the streams become dry washes. Korea is a forbidding country, plagued by human misery and blessed with little natural beauty.

It is particularly ironic that this nearly destitute country has for a long time been the battleground of great rival powers. Contending armies pillaging the countryside, spoiling the land with gunfire, have periodically set back Korea's slight chance for a satisfactory living standard.

For many years before World War II Korea had been the vassal of Japan. After Japan's defeat, the United States for the first time took a direct hand in trying to prepare Korea for an independent existence. To do this, the United States had to deploy troops there, but it had no intention of staying for long, or of guaranteeing the freedom of Korea indefinitely. The object was to give the Koreans a start, then get out and let them work out their own future.

By 1948, the withdrawal of American troops was well along. Armed units had been recalled to the United States. There remained in Seoul, the capital city, only a body of U. S. military trainers, called MAAG, whose job it was to instruct the Republic of Korea Army. Military leaders of the United States had already decided that the United States would not fight for Korea and would in the future avoid becoming involved in war anywhere on the Asiatic mainland.

So how did it happen that the United States became South Korea's champion, sacrificed thousands of American lives to keep that poor little land free, and how is it that the United States is today committed to fight again if any other power tries to overwhelm Korea? To find the whole explanation, it is necessary to review what happened to Korea during recent centuries.

One hundred years before Columbus discovered America, the Koreans, an extraordinarily homogeneous race with no minority groupings, came under the rule of the Yi dynasty, or family. This family ruled Korea well into the 1900's. During those years, at the turn of the sixteenth century, Japan invaded Korea and occupied it for seven years before it was driven out.

For many years the Ming rulers of China exercised some authority over Korea, treating it as a friendly dependent. The two peoples had religious ties (Buddhism and the Confucian moral code), and the Koreans did not find this rather loose political association oppressive. Things changed, however, when the Chinese Manchus overthrew the Mings in 1627, invaded and occupied Korea, and forced the Yi dynasty to submit to their dictates. For the first time Korea lost its independence. It was then that the little country declared its isolation from world society and won the name, "The Hermit Kingdom."

When Ivan the Terrible established himself as the first czar of the Russians in 1530, he rapidly expanded the Russian Empire to the eastward through Siberia. Other czars followed his lead. By 1644, Russian explorers had reached the Pacific. One century later, they were moving down the west coast of America. (Their penetration of California brought about the Monroe Doctrine.) The Russians also pushed southward from Siberia, and in 1860 China was forced to cede them her Maritime Province. Russia's boundary was now next to Korea.

Through its continuing expansion, Russia was finally face to face with Japan. Both countries hungrily eyed Korea, the stepping-stone between their national boundaries. But Japan, though rising rapidly as a modern military power, was not yet ready for a showdown.

Then, in 1896, the Japanese murdered the Korean queen, seized King Yi Tae-wang, and forced him to name a cabinet friendly to Japanese interests. The king then found sanctuary in the Russian embassy and ruled from there. After this checkmate, both powers backed away, signed a proclamation affirming Korean "independence," and withdrew their troops.

Japan speeded her military buildup. The czar's army and navy, ill led and riddled with court politics, was in bad shape, and growing worse. On February 8, 1904, with no warning, a Japanese squadron attacked the Russians at Port Arthur; next, the Japanese army landed in Korea, advanced rapidly to the northern frontier, and whipped the Russians in the Battle of the Yalu. It was the first shock notice to the world that Japan had arrived as a front-rank power. The war lasted into mid-1905. Russia was beaten everywhere. At the end, Korea was made a Japanese "protectorate," which word gave it at least the appearance of independence. That fiction ended in 1910, when Japan overthrew the last Korean king, Yi Hyeng, and formally annexed his country.

The Japanese maintained complete dominion in Korea for thirty-five years. Koreans became third-class citizens in their own country. The menial tasks were theirs. Children were taught Japanese in the schools, instead of their own tongue. Young men were drafted for labor battalions in the Japanese army. Most of Korea's present-day industrial plants, railways, port facilities, and highways were built by the Japanese with money wrung from the Korean people.

For these tokens of progress, the people paid an exorbitant price; through one-third century of total servitude, they forgot almost completely how to manage their own affairs. Along the fringes of Korea, various guerrilla leaders, like Kim Il Sung, struck back in revolt; but it was like a gnat going after a tiger. Liberty-loving young Koreans, among them one Lee Sung Man, who changed his name to Syngman Rhee, preferred exile abroad, where they tried to interest friendly governments in the cause of Korean independence. But when the opportunity at last came, the Koreans were not ready for it. Official Washington was well aware throughout the years of World War II that the Koreans were politically immature and would not be able to manage their own affairs. It was agreed that they must be tutored and protected for a long time before they could assume absolute responsibility for their own government. But Washington's plans for Korea were soon undone by Communist cunning.

UNATIONS

A Korean farmer's wife washes the family clothes in a stream.

The 38th Parallel

World War II ended in September, 1945, with the total surrender of Japan. Now little Korea, a bone without meat, was in paw reach of Russian armies that had turned against Japan in the last hour.

Dictator Joseph Stalin was all too well aware of Korea's value as a foil against Russia's traditional rivals, China and Japan, and as a checkmate to the United States which, having won the war in the Pacific, was bound to play a lead role in establishing the new order in Asia. He was set to overrun Korea, not to prepare it for freedom, but to convert it to Communism and thereafter exploit it. This had been his plan in Central Europe, where he had first liberated, then held captive, what are called the Iron Curtain countries.

In 1943, after the Cairo Conference, Stalin had agreed with U.S. policy that "in due course Korea shall be free and independent." But he was speaking tongue in cheek. When, near the end of World War II, President Roosevelt died, and Mr. Truman took office, Washington still believed that Russia had no sinister design toward Korea. At the Potsdam Conference in the summer of 1945, Mr. Truman and Stalin agreed that the main problem as to Korea was how the arrangements should be set to accept the Japanese surrender in that territory. The Russians were right at the border. The closest U.S. Army corps was in Okinawa, six hundred miles away. These two armies would divide the work; the question was how. Admiral Matthias Gardner of the United States pointed to the 38th Parallel, which crosses Korea in the middle, and asked: "Why not put the dividing line there?" Few words have led to more vast consequences.

On August 12, two days before Japan quit, 100,000 Russian soldiers under General Ivan Chistiakov invaded Korea and marched to the 38th Parallel. The U.S. XXIV Corps, under General John Hodge, shipped to Korea from Okinawa one month later. They found the Parallel already under guard and established as a sealed-off border. Behind it, the Russians were training North Korean youth to bear arms, bombarding the people with Communist propaganda, and installing Moscow-schooled Koreans in positions of power. They had no intention that Korea should ever again be united except under the Red Flag, and with their militant outlook, they believed that, in the end, this would come about.

The plan of the United States was to prepare the whole of Korea methodically for independence. When the Russians divided the land and its people, the only possible alternative for the United States was to try quickly to give the southern half of the country sufficient power and political know-how to endure. It had to make the best of Hobson's choice. Every effort by and through the United Nations to stage an election or plebiscite by which the Koreans might work out their own fate was spurned by Russia. The United States, therefore, set about training young men in South Korea to bear arms. Meanwhile, it thinned out its own garrison.

Far ahead of the time the United States had ever intended, ROK (Republic of Korea) independence was decreed, an election was held, and Dr. Syngman Rhee, now an aged man, was named first president.

Famine, plague, and joblessness would have taken over the new republic but for large and continuing grants of American aid. In the north, Russian forces finally pulled out, leaving behind a

North Korean Army, armed with Russian weapons and schooled to conduct war ruthlessly. One of its leaders was a new Kim Il Sung, Moscow-trained protégé of the old guerrilla chief. The Army of South Korea, under U.S. guidance, was trained and armed more for police work than for battle, and had few heavy weapons. All American field units were withdrawn from the country.

Such was the unstable, unsatisfactory balance of things in Korea as 1950 opened. Seoul and Washington knew very little of what was happening beyond the 38th Parallel because the Communists had closed the border between North and South Korea.

The sealing off of one part of the country from the other was only one of the penalties of artificially dividing a country that had been integrated throughout its history. Korea now faced economic hopelessness. All Korea's mineral wealth, power, and heavy industry are located mainly in the Communist North. South Korea has more agricultural abundance, schools of higher learning, and ports suitable to serve world commerce. United, the two halves of Korea would have a fighting chance to become self-sufficient. Divided, they are condemned to chronic invalidism. This heartless partitioning, more than the war of aggression, is the real tragedy fixed on Korea by the Communist ambition to dominate world affairs.

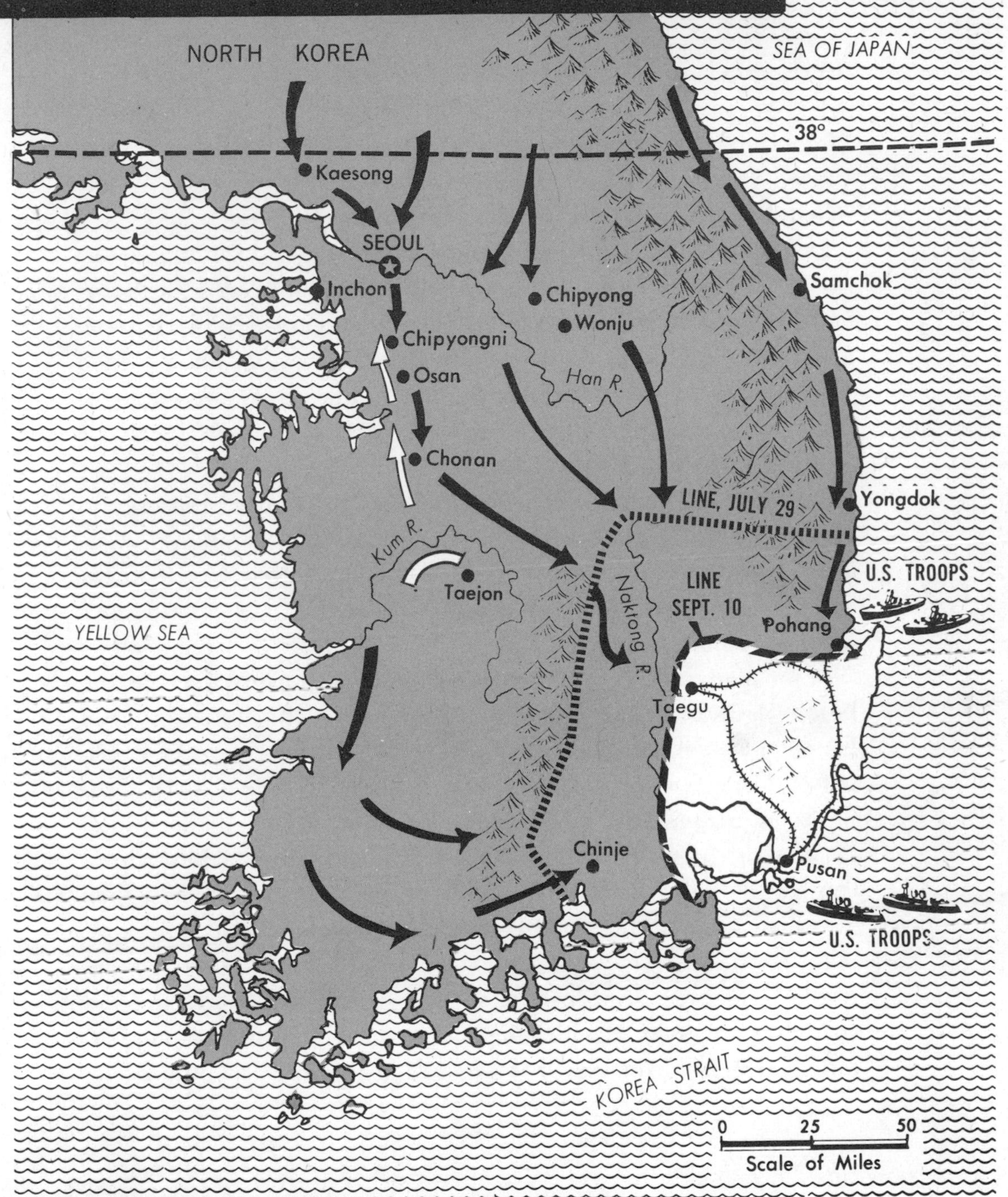

NORTH KOREAN ADVANCES—SUMMER 1950
NORTH KOREA
SEA OF JAPAN
38°
Kaesong
SEOUL
Inchon
Chipyong
Wonju
Samchok
Chipyongni
Osan
Han R.
Chonan
LINE, JULY 29
Yongdok
Kum R.
Taejon
Naktong R.
LINE
SEPT. 10
U.S. TROOPS
Pohang
YELLOW SEA
Taegu
Chinje
Pusan
U.S. TROOPS
KOREA STRAIT
0
25
50
Scale of Miles

War and Its Forces

THROUGH the first months of 1950, rumors sifted through to the United States that the North Korean Army was engaged in a massive military buildup, with intensified combat training.

In Tokyo, the Supreme Commander's chief of intelligence, Major General Charles Willoughby, U.S.A., pondered these rumors. Pieced together, his information convinced him that the Korean Communists were mounting an invasion force which would strike approximately at the beginning of summer, and his count showed within one division of the actual strength which the North Koreans were readying.

But Willoughby's secret warnings were discounted not only in his own headquarters but also in Washington official circles. Americans were optimistic; they could not believe that North Korea and Russia, its sponsor, would recklessly break their contract and loose unlimited violence.

Some part of this confidence was due to the presence of the heroic figure, General Douglas MacArthur, in the Far East, and his achievement as proconsul in taking a prostrate Japan and lifting it through reconstruction into newfound freedom, with prosperity in prospect. The U.S. Eighth Army, under the leadership of Lieutenant General Walton Walker, was at General MacArthur's command. This army was based on Japan, closer to Korea than any Russian main body. Its presence seemed reassuring. But two main considerations were overlooked. The Eighth Army was untried, formed of ill-trained draftees for the most part, and not structured for war. Each regiment had been stripped of one battalion, which meant that if it was called to fight, it would be in-

U.S. ARMY PHOTOGRAPH

Lieutenant General Walton H. Walker (left) confers with General William F. Dean at an advanced airfield in Korea.

flexible. There was also the mistaken belief on the part of the Communists that the United States had clearly indicated it would not intervene in a sideshow war in Asia. These were the fateful ingredients that dulled caution.

With both sides guessing wrong about the other's intentions, a planned Communist coup was blown up into an international war. In reality, the North Korean Army was so far superior to the South Korean that quick conquest was inevitable, if other nations kept hands off. During the first half of 1950, the NK Army doubled in size. It numbered 170,000 troops with 15 infantry and 2 armored divisions. Russia supplied its main heavy weapons — 150 sturdy T-34 tanks and 200 Yak (propeller-driven) fighter planes — without which there would have been no aggression. South Korea had no tanks, no military planes. The ROK Army of 98,000, like the National Police of 45,000, was armed chiefly with hand-carried weapons, such as rifles and carbines. Its eight infantry divisions were hollow shells, incapable of moving fast or resisting armored columns. Their higher officers had no battle command experience.

At 4 A.M. on June 25, a rainy Sunday morning, General Chai Ung Chai's Communist divisions struck into South Korea over six invasion routes. The defenders at the 38th Parallel were totally surprised and stunned; their well-wishers over the world were completely shocked. Immediately, Communist propaganda sounded the note that Chai's army had struck in self-defense to forestall invasion; it is a familiar Big Lie. South Korea was so far from being prepared to attack that its army was beaten at the frontier almost before the news of the attack got out. By midmorning of the first day, all six columns had broken through, overrun ROK outposts and destroyed main positions. At Kaesong, where one ROK division stood guard, the defense lasted three hours. There was no way to stop the tanks; besides, one NK regiment had ridden right into town aboard a freight train. On June 28, Seoul fell. The ROK government had already moved south to Taejon. American civilians were evacuated by way of the port of Inchon.

By the time the war was seven hours old, and the Communist army had cleaned up its first-day objectives, the United States State Department at last got the news. President Truman, off on a visit, was called at his family home in Independence, Missouri. He authorized Secretary of State Dean Acheson to request a meeting of the UN Security Council. When the Secretary General, Trygve Lie, heard the story, he exclaimed, "This is war against the United Nations." So it was. Next day, with ten members present, the Council voted to demand that the Communists cease fighting and return home. It was the absence of the eleventh member, Russia, who was boycotting UN in a sulk, that enabled this first step to be taken, thereby putting UN on the side of South Korea. Now back in Washington, Mr. Truman counseled with his chief military advisers and Secretary Acheson, then cabled General MacArthur to use Navy and Air Force to stop the Communists from capturing Seoul. It was already too late for that, but official Washington believed that once American forces landed in Korea, the North Koreans would lose heart and collapse. It also believed that if it restricted its military action to driving the Communists from South Korea, it could avoid a general war. The U.S. Seventh Fleet and Fifth Air Force (based on Japan) were the first to go to Korea, and Washington felt that not much more would be needed.

U.S. ARMY PHOTOGRAPH

The first units of U.S. Army Ground Forces debark from trains in South Korea.

Vainer, more wishful expectations cannot be imagined. On June 29, the day after Seoul fell, General MacArthur flew from Tokyo to Suwon, twenty miles south of Seoul, to see with his own eyes what was happening. What he saw persuaded him that by putting in only two of his own U.S. divisions to stiffen the demoralized ROK's, he could stop the North Koreans. Next day Mr. Truman cabled him authority to use Army forces. With that act, the United States became irrevocably committed; but its leaders were still thinking of the Communist invasion as a weekend war and were far underestimating the fighting power and tenacity of the North Koreans. Already, before the scope of the war could be measured, Britain, Australia, New Zealand, and Canada were volunteering to send forces, responding to a UN resolution to sponsor an army under its own flag. Eventually, sixteen nations contributed troops or direct assistance in some form to the South Koreans' fight for freedom. Yet in the beginning they, too, thought it would be easy. By the end, the labor, sacrifice, and supply help of a non-ally, Japan, probably sustained the U.S. war effort more than all else.

On June 30, two rifle battalions of the U.S. 24th Infantry Division were airlifted from Kyushu, Japan, to Pusan in Korea. Major General William F. Dean temporarily commanded the small expedition. One U.S. battalion went into position at Osan, seven miles below Suwon, and was hit and routed by superior forces. The U.S. guns were too light to penetrate the T-34 tanks with which Russia had supplied North Korea. Three days later the other U.S. battalion was beaten at Chonan. It was already clear that the North Koreans were rushing for Pusan and a smash ending to the war. For the first time, the United States and its allies believed that the Communists might make it.

By July 13, two regiments of the 24th Division had formed a defense line along the Kum River. On the same day, the 25th Division landed at Pusan, and General Walker, leader of the U.S. Eighth Army, was named commander of all UN soldiers in Korea. Two days later, three Communist divisions broke through and rode around the twenty-mile front that the Americans had formed on the Kum. Next, the Americans tried to stand at Taejon; the battle for that city opened haltingly and lasted four days. At the end, on July 21, General Dean was cut off from his troops while trying to break out of Taejon with a rear guard, and eventually was taken prisoner. His bravery in battle won him the Medal of Honor, an honor certified by his courageous resistance to his Communist captors for three years. Many Americans regard him as the outstanding heroic figure of the Korean War.

The sixteen-day delaying action by the unaided 24th Division cost a thousand American lives, but it interrupted the Communist pell-mell advance and won precious days while fresh forces were

A 2½-ton truck tows a 105mm howitzer up to the front in an early-dawn move.

UNATIONS

U.S. ARMY PHOTOGRAPH

Members of the 17th Field Artillery Battalion fire an 8-inch howitzer at North Korean tanks.

on the way. Yet one NK column was in the clear and running unopposed down the west coast. After Taejon fell, the enemy offensive broadened. Eight divisions formed four main columns. Of the other three, one struck down the east coast toward Pohang, another advanced through the central mountain passes toward Taegu, and the last reached for that city via the main highway from Taejon. Seven additional NK divisions were either in reserve or moving up. By now, the NK Yaks had either been destroyed or driven from the skies by the United States Air Force and carrier-based planes. The main drag on Communist movement overland was a chronic shortage of fuel for tanks and truck convoys. Fully occupied with their own deployments, the Americans as yet were

U.S. ARMY PHOTOGRAPH

United Nations troops fire white phosphorus into a Communist-held position while elements of the 35th Infantry Regiment, 25th Division, keep a sharp lookout for any movement of Communist forces.

doing nothing to reorganize or suitably arm the badly broken ROK Army; General Walker controlled its parts on the battlefield, but President Rhee otherwise retained command of them.

Atrocities and mass human misery already gave extra dimension to the war's terror. Americans and ROK's taken prisoner were sometimes tortured, tied hand and foot in groups and then shot in the back of the head. As the Communists descended on a countryside, thousands of refugees fled before them. These tragic columns were formed largely of aged people, little children, babes in arms, the crippled and helpless, all shuffling along together. They were without food, often without water. Many of them died in roadside ditches. They were a common sight until the war's end.

But there was grimness elsewhere, too. Though additional forces, already under arms, were being rushed from the United States, that country, despite the early defeats, went along for the most part business-as-usual. It was not put on a war footing. Defense Secretary Louis Johnson, pursuing a private quarrel with Secretary Acheson, forbade discussions of the war with the State Department. Having ordered widespread economies in all services shortly before the war began, Secretary Johnson stubbornly held to this course even while events in Korea made it clear that shortages were proving disastrous. For one thing, the United States had scrapped its minesweepers after World War II, and now it had to borrow some from its late enemy, Japan. Military leaders groaned from these self-inflicted wounds, but for the time being they could not cure them.

On July 18, the U.S. 1st Cavalry Division, out of Japan, landed at Pohang and advanced westward to join with the other Americans already fighting on the "northwest" front beyond Kumchon. Other reinforcements were on their way from Okinawa, Hawaii, and home bases. They landed at Pusan in the first days of August — one brigade from the 1st Marine Division, two regiments of the 2nd Infantry Division, two regimental combat teams from the Pacific islands, and one Marine air wing. These were all the troops that General Walker was to get for his first decisive battle and, including the five badly shaken ROK divisions, they counted less than 100,000 men.

In driving west from Pohang, the cavalry division was trying to form a defensive wedge shielding southeast Korea and blocking the Communists from that area. Though its rearward detachments were too thin to withstand any heavy attack, they were extended

UNATIONS

A Korean farmer carries his wife to the refugee camp near Kimhae.

along the line that had to be held. This line formed a triangle whose points were Taegu, the new, temporary capital of South Korea, and the port cities of Pusan and Pohang. All three cities were connected by railroad. If they could be held, there was still space and time to permit the UN force buildup and recovery while at the same time frustrating the Communist plan to gather in all Korea and destroy the foreigners.

One strong geographical feature of Korea was in the favor of the United Nations forces. Through South Korea, the wide Naktong River runs mainly north and south, passing Taegu and Pusan on the westward. This barrier, and the broad valley running from Taegu to Pohang, defined the defensive front called the "Pusan Perimeter." The enclosed area was about forty-five by eighty-five miles, and the irregular defensive front was roughly two hundred miles.

On August 31, ten days after they had captured Taejon, the Communists got Chinju, fifty miles west of Pusan. Another Communist column captured Kumchon. The Communists then attacked Pohang, and for seven days thereafter the battle flamed all around the perimeter. Hard beset from north and west, all United Nations forces fell back gradually to the critical Pusan Perimeter. Twice the Communists took Pohang, and twice the United Nations troops recaptured the city. Now Taegu came under Communist artillery fire. The Naktong defense line was repeatedly broken, then made whole again by limited United Nations counterattacks east of the river. Along the south coast the Communists, driving east, got within twenty-eight miles of Pusan. The U.S. bombers, based on Japan, quit attacking main targets in North Korea to provide direct support to the hard-pressed infantry in southeast Korea.

The prolonged struggle around the vital perimeter developed

as a series of bitterly fought local engagements. Short of fuel, lacking dependable communications, the Communists simply could not coordinate a combined offensive employing all forces at one time. Superior mobility and the limited spread of the fighting front worked for the Americans and made their patchwork tactics good enough. On September 7, the first non-American UN forces, two battalions of British infantry, went into position along the Naktong. In the next week the Communists staged their heaviest attack on Taegu and almost got it. But at midmonth the situation was little changed. The Communists could not smash the perimeter. UN forces could not break out of it. No major change appeared imminent.

Back in the United States, not even a semimobilization had been declared, though already some reservists were being called up. Public clamor against Secretary Johnson's inaction was about to retire him. His place would be taken by the old soldier, General George C. Marshall. Many American newspapers were saying that the people were indifferent to the war. But that was not true. While war is never popular with the American people, they stood ready to see this one through to a successful finish. However, many of their leaders viewed it fearfully, worrying that it would spread and too deeply involve the United States.

UNATIONS

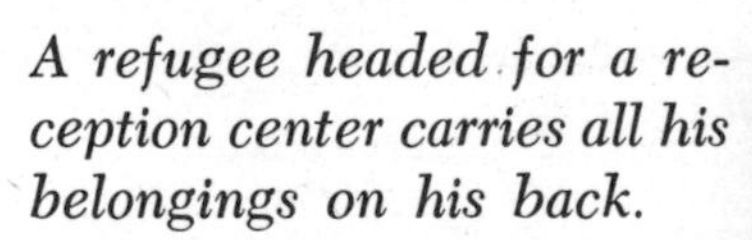

A refugee headed for a reception center carries all his belongings on his back.

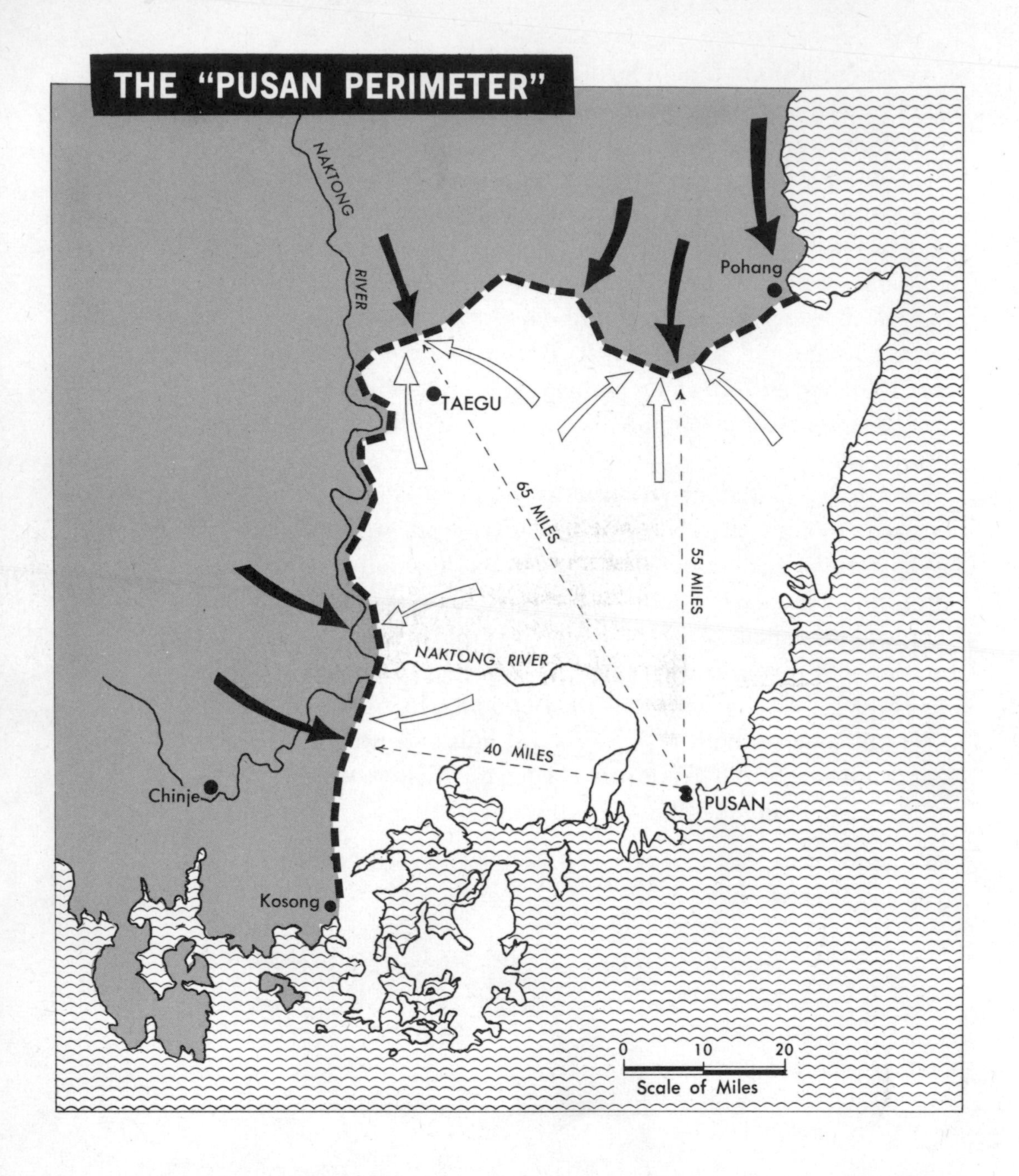
THE "PUSAN PERIMETER"
NAKTONG
RIVER
Pohang
TAEGU
65 MILES
55 MILES
NAKTONG RIVER
40 MILES
Chinje
PUSAN
Kosong
0
10
20
Scale of Miles

Illusion of Victory

SINCE mid-July General MacArthur had been planning the grand maneuver to break the deadlock in the battle for Pusan and free General Walker's army to move again. As Supreme Commander, he was responsible for the strategy, and he had decided on the kind of operation best suited to his genius and daring. He had used this same operation repeatedly in his advance from Australia back to the Philippines in World War II — a surprise thrust deep into the enemy rear by the combined services. The U.S. Navy's absolute command of the sea made it possible.

On September 15, another U.S. expedition, formed of a separate army corps in Japan and attacking out of Navy transports, fought its way ashore at Inchon, the main port serving Seoul, 150 miles north of the Pusan battle. The expedition was under Vice Admiral Arthur D. Struble, who led the U.S. Seventh Fleet; two reinforced U.S. divisions — 7th Infantry and 1st Marine — formed X Corps, under Major General Edward M. (Ned) Almond. By this time, half-trained Korean soldiers (called Katusas) were being used to fill out the American infantry units, due to the shortage of U.S. riflemen on hand.

General MacArthur's maneuver was a stunning success. U.S. troops captured Inchon the first day. From there, General Almond's corps drove east and south to block the approaches to Seoul, which was defended by one NK division. One column of Marines captured Yongdungpo, an industrial suburb south of the Han River; the other seized Kimpo Airfield. Two days later that base was unloading military cargo flown from Japan. The U.S. 7th Division, landing behind the Marines, drove on to Suwon, and took the city and its airfield on September 22.

Until that day, the Communist army along the Pusan Perimeter had stood its ground and fought back, ignoring the explosion on its rear. Then in an hour, it evaporated; its people disappeared north and west through the hills. By motor, the 1st Cavalry Division sped north and on September 26 joined hands with the advance guard of the 7th Division at Osan, where Americans had fought the first battle. In the south, the 25th and 2nd Divisions raced toward the west coast, and the 24th Division drove for Taejon. This spreading net bagged thousands of Communist prisoners. But the U.S. lines were too thinly manned, and thousands more Communist soldiers sifted through and escaped north. No one believed at the time that their escape would cost the United Nations dear. On September 26 Seoul fell to General Almond's troops after a block-to-block defense by its die-hard garrison. The capitol and other main buildings were burned out and made useless, though government moved back and resumed work while the city still smoked.

To Koreans, the UN command, and the world, it looked as if the decisive battle were over and final victory within reach. Official Washington held that view, and because of it, suddenly became less cautious about withholding forces from Communist country. At the same time, and for the same reason, it became more casual about strengthening the war effort. Government first debated whether to invade North Korea, then passed the decision to General MacArthur.

In Korea, Dr. Rhee was playing a forcing hand. By October 1, on the east coast, two of his ROK divisions, taking orders from him, were already across the 38th Parallel, while another column,

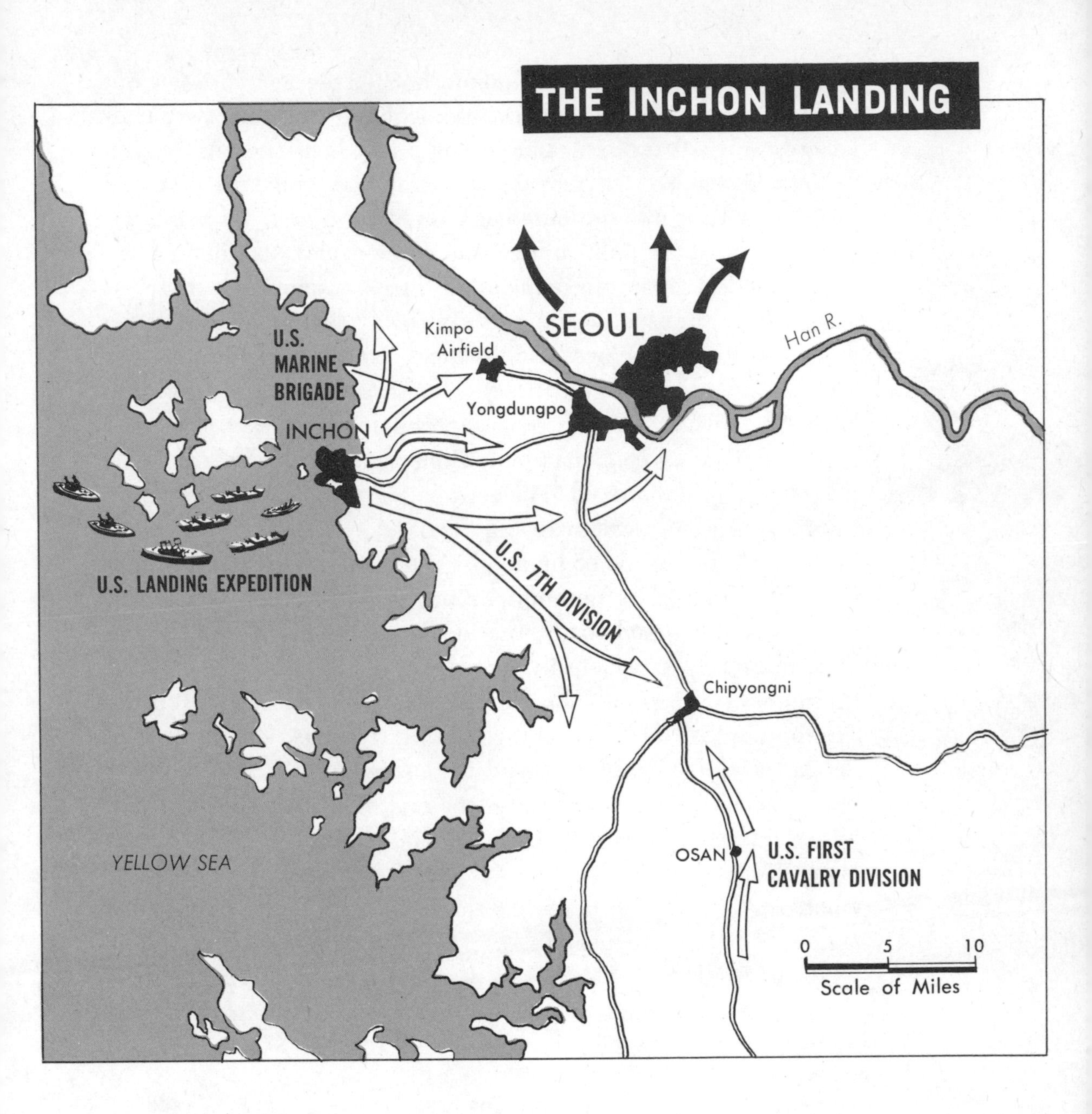
THE INCHON LANDING
SEOUL
Han R.
Kimpo
Airfield
U.S.
MARINE
BRIGADE
Yongdungpo
INCHON
U.S. LANDING EXPEDITION
U.S. 7TH DIVISION
Chipyongni
OSAN
U.S. FIRST
CAVALRY DIVISION
YELLOW SEA
0
5
10
Scale of Miles

marching through Seoul, was bound not for the near frontier but the Yalu River. The first Americans, a column from the 1st Cavalry, crossed the parallel near Kaesong a few hours before the UN General Assembly, in New York, voted that MacArthur should proceed with a mop-up campaign in North Korea. In this way, soldiers forced the political decision while diplomats debated.

Still under separate command, General Almond's corps was loaded onto ships at Inchon and carried by the Navy around the peninsula to make a sweep of northeast Korea. The Marine division landed unopposed at Wonsan on October 25, and four days later the 7th Division was put ashore at Iwon. In fact, the coast was so quiet that comedian Bob Hope was on hand to welcome troops when they arrived. The area had already been mopped up by the ROK divisions advancing overland.

This splitting of the command by General MacArthur was later roundly criticized as unsound military practice, but because of Korea's lack of good roads, the move was essential if all forces were to be kept satisfactorily supplied. (Washington's estimate of the number of supplies that would be needed was based on the assumption that the worst of the fighting was over. Troops did not yet have winter equipment and cold weather was almost due.) No one knew beyond doubt that the end of the war was in sight, but optimism was running high. When, as UN forces drove into North Korea, there came a veiled warning from Foreign Minister Chou En-lai that Red China might enter the war, few American leaders took the threat seriously.

While the U.S. X Corps took its boat ride around Korea, the Eighth Army columns marched tediously north, more hampered by supply problems than by fire from NK soldiers fighting as small hit-and-run groups. There was no vestige of organized resistance among the Communists. American soldiers threw away their steel helmets, grenades, and other impedimenta as they marched, confident that there would be no more hard combat. This was due to inexcusably bad discipline, but American officers also had been made careless by fatigue and illusory success.

On October 6, one ROK battalion reached the Yalu. Shortly before its arrival, nine Chinese soldiers had come through the hills and voluntarily surrendered to a ROK headquarters. It was the first appearance of Chinese soldiers in the war. To intelligence officers they told this strange tale — that they were former Nationalists who had been forced into "volunteering" for units that would fight with the North Koreans. Until the end, Communist China maintained the fiction that its troops were not officially present.

Residents of Wonsan, in North Korea, pick their way through the wreckage of the city.

ASSOCIATED PRESS WIREPHOTO

This first sign of a new intervention left no hint of its scope or purpose. General MacArthur, meeting President Truman at Wake Island, assured him that the Red Chinese could not get enough troops into North Korea to block the victory march. That was the general opinion everywhere. General Willoughby, the intelligence chief in Tokyo, was an exception. He held a directly opposite view.

Swiftly, the air chilled. On its first night bivouac at the Yalu, the ROK battalion was trapped and butchered. The few survivors said Chinese had done it. On October 27 and 28, other ROK units near the river were ambushed and massacred. This had to be the work of new, well-organized forces. Sped north to support the badly demoralized ROK's (Korean soldiers have a superstitious awe of the Chinese), one squadron of the 1st Cavalry Division was ambushed near Unsan and nearly wiped out. Again, the enemy was Chinese. Eighth Army Intelligence, piecing together fragments of information, concluded that somewhere between thirty and sixty thousand Chinese had already crossed into Korea.

General Walker did not wait for this grim warning from his staff. He was a stiff-backed soldier who accepted orders with no questions, even when he did not agree with them, but the fight at Unsan had convinced him that the piecemeal advance to the Yalu by his army risked disaster. He ordered his troops farthest north to retire and re-form along the line of the Chongchon River which flows west to the Yellow Sea forty-five miles north of Pyongyang, the Communist capital. There, on the south bank, unopposed, the Eighth Army collected, received replacements, and reoutfitted during the next three weeks. In northeast Korea, General Almond's corps, meeting only fragmentary opposition, continued its advance toward the Yalu. It was the quietest period of the war. Only the headquarters of the Eighth Army thought the outlook ominous.

It was worse than this brooding staff guessed. Unseen, and almost unsuspected, the main body of the new enemy lay in hiding just across the river. In aggregate strength of 100,000 men, the 38th, 39th, and 40th Chinese Communist armies had secretly crossed into Korea. They traveled by night, to avoid being seen from the air. What supplies the soldiers did not themselves carry came along mainly on the backs of coolie laborers. The troops had no tanks and few field guns. But they were well fitted with grenades, rifles, tommy guns, machine guns, and mortars, and they were especially skilled with these last three weapons. They had learned their new tactics mainly by watching the Japanese in World War II. Also, they had divined what the Americans would do and had so deployed their strength that they would hit the American forces where they were weakest. Arriving opposite the Eighth Army, they concealed themselves in the Korean villages amid the hills. Packed in like sardines, a whole rifle company could thus be hid to view from the air by the roof of one hut. The essence of the surprise lay in their willingness to do things that Western soldiers would not dream of doing.

General Walker feared that somewhere before him lay a formidable enemy army, but just where or how big it was he did not know. General MacArthur, his superior, had no such premonition. On November 20 he ordered the Eighth Army to attack on a broad front the day after Thanksgiving, November 25. The public communiqué announcing the plan said: "This morning the western sector of the pincers (General Almond's corps being the eastern sector) moves forward in general assault in an effort to complete the compression and close the vise." General Almond's columns still advanced along parallel roads toward the border. There was a thirty-mile gap between the flanks of the field army and the independent corps, and they had only fragmentary radio contact. As General Willoughby was to comment two days later: "You must admit that this is a most unusual situation in war."

Two U.S. soldiers gaze across the Yalu River to the mountains of Manchuria.

U.S. ARMY PHOTOGRAPH

Great Defeat

On Thanksgiving Day, 1950, U.S. frontline soldiers in Korea dined on roast turkey, pumpkin pie, and all the "trimmings." They were grateful for these luxuries, not knowing that they were more in need of steel helmets and extra ammunition. Their normal appetites were whetted by high command assurance that they would wrap up the fighting and be home in time for Christmas.

Next morning they stepped out briskly on the new offensive. Throughout that day, the front of the Eighth Army rolled along, stopped only in three narrow company sectors. Yet these small blocks deserved more respectful attention than they got. A local, determined resistance by an entrenched enemy in broad daylight was unprecedented during the advance into North Korea. These small fights signaled a radically changed situation. American soldiers, finding fresh horse manure in the vicinity, had come to the conclusion that they had encountered Chinese forces. But because full information was not sent back, then correlated by higher headquarters, the significance of the three skirmishes went unnoted.

When the Eighth Army called a halt just before dark, and the rifle companies formed perimeters on the ridgetops for night defense, two of these enemy salients held solid. As dark closed down, a Chinese maneuver army, until then concealed in the watershed between the Chongchon and Kuryong rivers, launched a skillfully prepared counteroffensive. The entrenched works which the Eighth Army had run into early in the day were only trip wires designed to alert this maneuver army and get it in movement.

The Chinese attack was a complete surprise. The full-armed

U.S. ARMY PHOTOGRAPH

A seemingly endless column of South Korean refugees plod through the snow south of Kanmung.

blow fell heaviest on the ROK II Corps and the U.S. 2nd and 25th Divisions. Positioned on the open flank of the army, the Koreans were broken and dispersed in one night. The gate to the army's rear was now open to the enemy. One Chinese brigade cut straight through the 2nd Division, moving at a run in column. In four days of battle, the valorous 2nd lost 80 per cent of its people and nearly all of its guns. Though the 25th Division was formed with its regiments roughly in column when the Chinese hit, the enemy broke through to the artillery positions on the first night.

These and other blows which swiftly followed proved irreparable. The Turkish Brigade, making its first appearance in the war, was overrun and scattered by Chinese pouring through the gap where ROK II Corps had been. The British 27th Brigade and the

1st Cavalry Division were mauled while covering the withdrawal of the stricken forces. By November 28 the Eighth Army was wholly turned south with the Chinese in pursuit at the rate of about six miles per day, and the danger of a general envelopment was not yet ended. It was one of the great defeats, and also the longest retreat, in the history of U.S. forces.

Nor was the other half of the divided command spared. The independent corps paid no less heavily for the risk involved in the split. At first, it continued its march northward after the Eighth Army was struck. Its secondary column on the extreme right, proceeding from Iwon, reached the Yalu at Hyesanjin but found no enemy, except the bitter cold. The temperature had dropped to 30 degrees below zero. On November 20, near Koto, the Marine advance guard of the main column captured a few Chinese soldiers who said that an entrapment awaited the whole command when the lead regiments got to Yudam-ni, west of the Chosin Reservoir. Little heed was given this information because the Chinese informers were enlisted men. By nightfall of November 28, three days after the Eighth Army was split, the advance guard arrived at Yudam-ni. As yet it had seen no Communist troop bodies, but only a few small patrols. Units of the 7th Division, mainly artillery, were east of the reservoir. One commando group of British marines, with one battalion of U.S. Marines, escorted by tanks, was marching from Koto to Hagaru. Other 1st Marine Division perimeters were at Hagaru, Koto, and Chinhung. The distance from head to tail was fifty-three miles. Behind the last Marine battalion, the newly arrived U.S. 3rd Infantry Division had its front.

Within two hours after dark, every part of the far-extended U.S. forces was hit, and every perimeter north of the 3rd Division

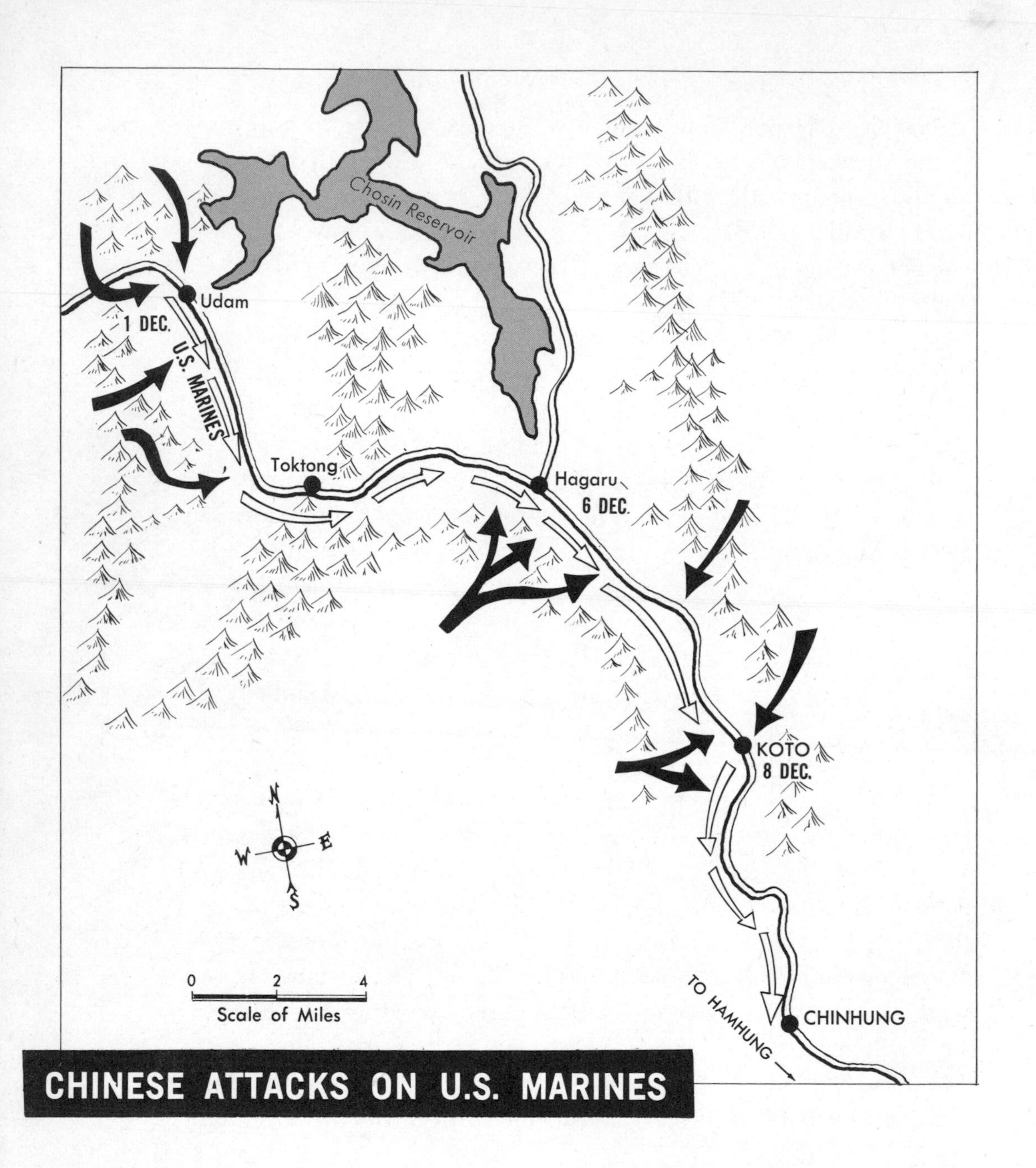

CHINESE ATTACKS ON U.S. MARINES

was almost simultaneously put under siege. A new Chinese army seemed to arise right out of the ground. East of the lake the American units were wiped out. Elsewhere, American troops successfully defended their positions, though all offensive prospects were ended immediately. When General Almond ordered the two Marine regiments at Yudam-ni to attack west and relieve pressure on the Eighth Army, obedience to these orders proved impossible, and the commanders said so. All components of the overstretched division were embattled, under fire from six Chinese divisions. The only question was whether they could survive; their one chance was to collect forces and attempt a breakout. Here, too, both sides suffered from the Arctic cold and deep snows. Enemy soldiers froze stiff in their trenches but feebly worked their weapons till the last. Icing stopped the U.S. weapons and cut firepower by half. More than 2,500 Marines became casualties to the weather.

On the other front, the Eighth Army, fighting rearguard actions as it moved, attacked repeatedly in night defense. Burning such of its supplies and equipage as hampered its movement, it fell back by slow stages to South Korea. The last of its troops crossed into friendly country on December 23. On that same day, General Walker was killed when his jeep skidded on an iced pavement while traveling at high speed. Lieutenant General Matthew B. Ridgway, one of the most courageous commanders from World War II, was flown from the United States to replace him. Earlier, it might have been possible to make a firm decision to stand on Seoul and the line of the Han River, risking a decisive battle while saving the capital from a second sacking. Now it was too late.

Final disaster had been averted in the independent corps largely because of the steadiness and wisdom of a great Marine com-

General Douglas MacArthur (left) confers with General John B. Colter.

ASSOCIATED PRESS WIREPHOTO

mander, Major General Oliver Smith. Fighting all the way, but timing his moves so that he could rest his troops between battles, General Smith brought his division and the remnants of the 7th back to the zone held by the 3rd Division. There, on December 10, the pressure eased as all forces neared the coast. Off the port of Hamhung, a 193-ship UN fleet awaited. An armed perimeter was thrown around Hamhung, covered by field weapons, air power, and naval gunfire. The evacuation operation started on December 12, and ended December 24. Three U.S. divisions, two ROK divisions, 91,000 Korean civilians, 17,300 vehicles, and 350,000 tons of supply were brought off. The gradually contracting beachhead was never penetrated by the enemy.

On December 27, U.S. X Corps was made part of the Eighth Army, terminating the split command arrangement which had compromised the November operations. Three weeks before his death, General Walker had urged this change on General MacArthur. General Walker's successor got the benefit of it. General

MacArthur ceased the close supervision he had previously exercised over all forces, and General Ridgway was given complete authority to plan and execute operations in Korea.

As the year ended, the Eighth Army abandoned Seoul and Kimpo Airfield, after another bonfire of nonmovable supply. The withdrawal finally ended near Osan. On New Year's Day, the Chinese resumed their attack. They took Seoul and Suwon, got past Wonju in the peninsula's center, and approached Samchok on the east coast. On this, their high-water mark, the offensive ended due to shortage of supply and human energy. Like other armies, the Chinese Reds had mortal limitations.

But it was easy to forget that the Chinese were human while they still rolled forward. In fact, General MacArthur warned the Joint Chiefs of Staff that the Chinese armies could, if they wished, drive the UN forces out of Korea, which grim view gave the Chinese far too much credit. But understandably, the shock from the defeat was tremendous and it carried far. In America, an unjustified optimism changed almost overnight to an equally unwarranted

U.S. ARMY PHOTOGRAPH

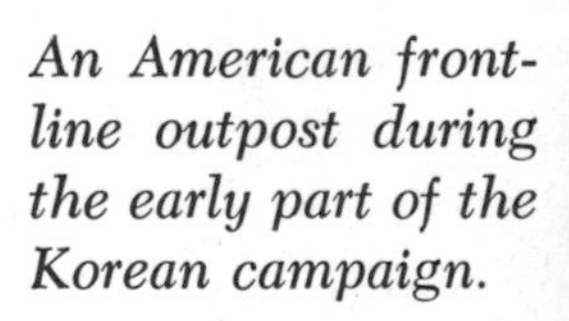

An American front-line outpost during the early part of the Korean campaign.

OFFICIAL PHOTOGRAPH, U.S. NAVY

Trucks of the 1st Marine Division in retreat from the Choisin Reservoir sector.

pessimism — the feeling that nothing could be saved. Markedly, this same despairing reaction occurred in higher commands and mighty seats outside of Korea. For many weeks the decision-making power in the highest levels of government and at UN was virtually paralyzed. Only the silence was impressive. No great man spoke majestic phrases either of cheer or of defiance. None said: "This is what we will do. We will fight on. We will redouble our effort. We will never give up."

Soldiers in Korea, whipped, forced to give ground, bodily weary, hungered for such words. They at least had given a good account of themselves, and fought bravely, though many false news stories out of Korea branded them a runaway army. So it was not one of the nobler chapters in American history, and nothing but the fortitude of the average fighting man redeemed it.

UNATIONS

U.S. Marines move forward after their units have bombed enemy positions on a Korean hillside.

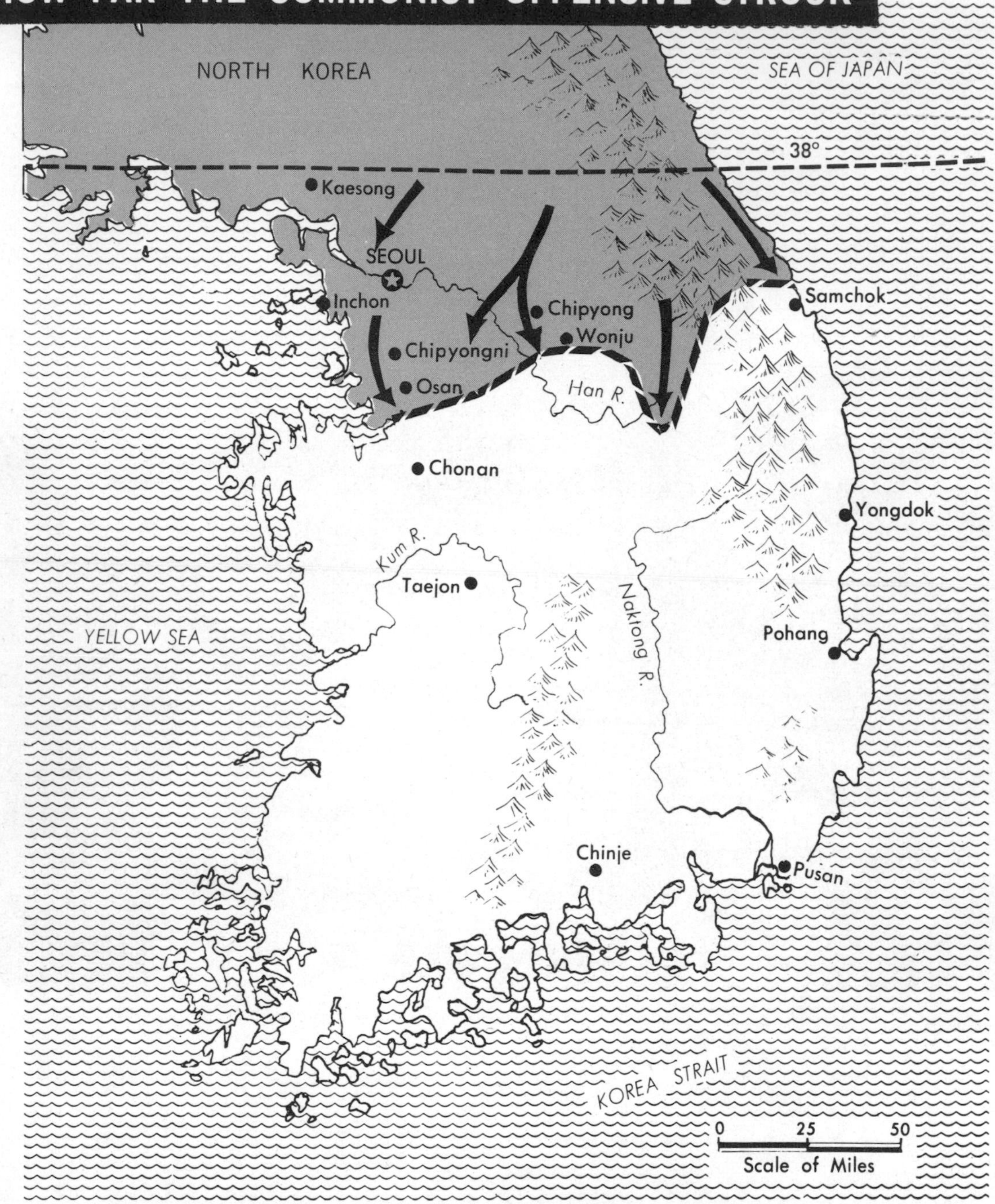
HOW FAR THE COMMUNIST OFFENSIVE STRUCK
NORTH KOREA
SEA OF JAPAN
38°
Kaesong
SEOUL
Inchon
Chipyong
Wonju
Chipyongni
Osan
Han R.
Samchok
Chonan
Yongdok
Kum R.
Taejon
Naktong R.
YELLOW SEA
Pohang
Chinje
Pusan
KOREA STRAIT
0
25
50
Scale of Miles

Peculiar War

For Americans who fought, it was a peculiar war, and the bizarre look was there even in that first January, 1951, when the two sides drew apart, the UN forces to recoup, the Communists because inertia and supply shortage gripped them.

This pause in the battle, though hardly anyone sensed it at the time, was the first symptom of the condition that made the ultimate stalemate. The United States had too few divisions present to maintain steady offensive pressure when its troops were deep in enemy country; the Chinese had abundant manpower reserves but lacked modern transportation. When they deployed into South Korea, they were too far from their Manchurian bases to keep their front line fixed with ammunition and defensive material — heavy timbers, sandbags, and improvised mines. In contrast to the shallow American foxholes, they chose to fight out of strong-walled, deep bunkers.

Due to exaggerated fear that the Chinese might keep coming, and the expedition would have to make a final desperate stand around Pusan, the United States made a study on how to use the atomic bomb as a last resort. But no decision was ever taken, and none was needed, for the Pusan nightmare soon lifted.

In extraordinary variety, though still in small numbers, military units from Europe, Southeast Asia, and the Antipodes, kept arriving in Japan and Pusan to help the UN side. Each contingent had its own national and religious customs, with requirements and taboos regarding diet and other things. These had to be respected. As the new troops took their place in line under General Ridgway, his staff officers undertook to solve these multifarious and complex problems so that there would be no undue strain on the comradeship of the international army. That they achieved their goal was one of the truly happy results of the UN's intervention in the Korean crisis. No multination army throughout history ever fought together in higher spirit and with less friction.

American infantrymen who were on duty manning the outposts along the ridgetops took frostbitten fingers and toes for granted, but even those who were not on sentry duty had the problem of beating the intense cold. They solved it by moving in with Korean farm families, though the average home was warm only right next to the fire. The United Nations soldiers made themselves welcome by sharing their food, fuel, and clothing with their new friends. If the children were ill, or the mother needed help, the troops looked after them. Amid great deprivation, the touch of human nature was present everywhere. U.S. combat units picked up Korean war orphans to serve as mascots and dressed them in cut-down GI uniforms with NCO (noncommissioned officer) chevrons. Korean schools had to be vacated so that they could be taken over for headquarters by a division or regiment. Staff problems were worked out on blackboards where kindergarten artwork still hung. It always surprised U.S. soldiers that the Korean schools were so poorly furnished. Most of the equipment was handmade. Where

ACME

Parentless refugee children who have been airlifted to a school building near Chiju City.

they could, when they vacated, the American soldiers left some supplies that might help. The gentlest side of the GI's came out in their compassion toward the Koreans. The general misery and poverty of these people, the agonizing sight of the long refugee columns plodding through the snow, was the one impression of the Korean War that outlasted the worst personal hardship among the men who fought it.

Eighth Army itself was hurting for necessities. True enough, by mid-January, creature comforts were available. The Army was surfeited with winter clothing and goodies for the table — fresh meats and vegetables, even ice cream and, occasionally, beer. But such dire needs as motortrucks, barbed wire, engineering tools, and protective mines remained critically short. (There were only two searchlights in the theater, and the Army needed many for use in night defense.)

The Army did not have enough pioneer forces to keep roads in repair along the front. Because vehicles could not travel over the broken trails, troops going forward were burdened like pack animals. There was a way to solve this problem and it was done. More than 100,000 Korean men were formed into a service corps and given American pay to keep roads in repair and carry fighting supply to the front line, loaded on A-frames which fit on the human back.

On the Communist side, there was no shortage of willing backs. The wants of the Chinese Communist soldier were simple. His day's ration was a handful or so of rice or millet and maybe a little dried fish. That hand-labor-supplied army out of Manchuria now powered the enemy front. It was patched here and there by a reorganized NK battalion, but large formations of enemy Koreans did not again appear. From now on, the Chinese ran the show.

HRS-I Sikorsky helicopter drops a cargo net loaded with supplies on inaccessible terrain in Korea.

U.S. MARINE CORPS PHOTOGRAPH

General Ridgway, a commander of much more independent mind and personal magnetism than General Walker, breathed a new spirit into his army. So that he could better understand its problems, and encourage his soldiers, he spent most of his time far forward with his divisions. That made difficulties for his own staff in Taegu, but it was a small price to pay for the transformation he brought about among the men in line simply by his presence among them. He knew that this is the right way to lead Americans in battle, as did Washington, Grant, Patton, and other truly heroic figures from America's past.

At this same time another interesting development was taking place. Since the Civil War, American Negroes in the Army had been formed into solid units. In short, they were segregated. In the November-December fighting in Korea, certain battalions that had fought gloriously had become integrated by chance just before the action. Because of this, there arose in the Eighth Army an overpowering sentiment in favor of integration from flank to flank. It was due to this influence that a great national reform was at last brought about.

The Recovery

DURING January, 1951, there was deep patrolling by both sides. Some of the Chinese patrol activities swelled into fierce raids that dealt surprise death by night far behind the front lines. The raiders stole forward along stream beds and canals, struck swiftly, then vanished. But no great damage was done and even the heavy artillery rarely fired, for the enemy was beyond range. The stalemate continued. Full recovery by the Eighth Army seemed no more likely than that the Communists, having come so far south, could complete their sweep of the peninsula. Few of the generals were of the same opinion about what would happen when the fighting resumed full scale. It was the most mystifying period of the war. Except that the Air Force continued to hammer targets in North Korea, meeting opposition only when the planes flew close to the Manchurian border, both sides acted with extraordinary caution.

U.S. ARMY PHOTOGRAPH

Self-propelled 155-mm gun lights up the night sky in Korea.

U.S. ARMY PHOTOGRAPH

Elements of the 27th Infantry Regiment, 25th Infantry Division, continue their advance at Anyang-ni.

When the tide again ran, the turn was almost imperceptible. From near Osan, UN patrols scouted into Suwon and found the city unoccupied except for a few furtive skirmishes. Aware of their own weakness, the rest of the Chinese on this part of the front had pulled back to the ridges a few miles north. At once, Ridgway pushed U.S. I Corps, which held the left flank, into Suwon. From there, as February opened and bright weather, the first sign of spring in Korea, arrived, the U.S. I Corps started a limited offensive to drive the Communists back across the Han River. It was

U.S. ARMY PHOTOGRAPH

An infantry regiment stops to rest.

called "Operation Punch." It used fresh tactics daringly designed to suck back the Chinese by night into ground from which they had been driven by day, whereupon UN forces would surround and inflict severe casualties on them.

From this inspiration came the most efficient attack staged by the UN side during the whole Korean War, and the spectacular success was rightly timed to restore confidence after three months of unrelieved defeat. The battle developed around a great ridge called Hill 440. By the end of five days, the objectives had been

U.S. ARMY PHOTOGRAPH

An infantry regiment goes into action against the Chinese Communists southwest of Seoul.

won. While losing only 237 men killed and wounded, the Eighth Army counted more than 5,000 enemy dead on the battlefield. During one eddy in the fight, on a hill southwest of Seoul, the Americans drove home the heaviest bayonet charge since Cold Harbor in the Civil War. Ridgway had reinstituted training with this weapon, believing it helped aggressiveness. Certainly it struck fresh fear in the Chinese. After falling back on Seoul, they marked time and did not again venture across the river.

Gradually the UN front was brought up even with this first thrust to the river line. There was no great general battle in which all divisions attacked together. Rather, the Army lurched forward, one battalion or so hitting at a time, then holding its new sector until the flanks came up. At last, two corps stood abreast along the south bank of the Han. Inchon and Kimpo Airfield were taken again, seven weeks following the evacuation bonfires. In the U.S. X Corps zone, through four days in February, the Chinese launched one of their rare but overly publicized "human sea" attacks, in which hundreds of men, bunched close together, came on at a run. This happened at the village of Chipyong-ni in central Korea. The Chinese hit the newly arrived French battalion and one regiment of the rebuilt 2nd Division, which had taken the worst of the shock up north. This time the tables were turned. After grim, great slaughter, the Chinese pulled back and again ceased their attacks.

By early March, the whole Eighth Army front was relatively stable, and the flow of trained replacements and resupply became satisfactory. Other limited attacks by United States forces promptly followed. In some of these, Navy carrier-based aviation bombed and strafed ahead of the infantry. On March 14, UN troops reentered Seoul, never again to yield it. Continuing, the Eighth Army once more advanced its lines beyond the 38th Parallel in a series of pincers movements. But the closing was always a little

U.S. ARMY PHOTOGRAPH

An infantry division advances across rice paddies near Seoul.

late; eluding the traps, the Communists pulled away north.

Most of these actions were very similar in pattern. Almost invariably, the Communists attacked by night, hoping to achieve surprise and elude the outpost line, but intending mainly to strike when the Americans and South Koreans could not call on their close support aviation to hit back with bombs and napalm.

The defenders would be positioned in armed perimeters on a ridgetop, the men hunched low in their foxholes, usually in pairs. At the first sign of the enemy advance, usually the slight noise of men moving through loose rock or brush, the mortars of U.S. artillery were signaled to fire flares. In the attack, the Chinese came on erect, in successive thin lines of tommy gunners and grenadiers. In the light of the flares they were conspicuously silhouetted. If the lighting lasted, they ducked down and fought from behind the rocks, while their snipers wiggled forward. The Chinese were very clever at this; worming their way through the brush, they often managed to bring the machine guns to within less than twenty yards of the American front. The attack would persist until one side or the other ran out of ammunition, which frequently happened just before dawn.

The Americans, on the other hand, invariably attacked by day so as to take advantage of their air and artillery cover. Another reason was that the American soldiers found it difficult to stay together in night movement among the mazelike ridge patterns. The Chinese were usually positioned in deep, shell-resistant bunkers atop and along the faces of the ridges. These bunkers were so aligned that they covered the gentler slopes along the ridge ends. The Americans had to advance via these same slopes, but they stayed low, and advanced either crawling or in short rushes from

U.S. ARMY PHOTOGRAPH

Members of the 27th Infantry Regiment fire at a Chinese gun emplacement near Seoul.

The 1st Cavalry Division brings in prisoners east of Wonju.

U.S. ARMY PHOTOGRAPH

rock to rock. So narrow was the average ridge crest that in these attacks a company "front" might be wide enough for only a squad of men. The other squads would be coming on behind it and trying to help the front runners with their fire. While the infantry made this tediously slow approach, the UN fighter planes would try to kill the Chinese bunkers with bombs and napalm. But usually the rock overhang covered the firing slots so perfectly that heavier weapons could not get at them, and the infantry had to end the action with a closing rush.

Taking one hill was invariably a full day's work or more. Just before sundown, the Americans would break off action, form their defensive circle somewhere on the high ground, and prepare to stand for the night. They slept, if at all, a few winks at a time, their weapons in their hands. That was what made Korea such an exhausting war. There was never any time for rest, and no good place for it, save when a lucky soldier was flown out for a few days' leave in Japan.

So the character of the fighting during that winter and early spring was determined largely by the Eighth Army's great advantage in heavy weapons. The Communist front had only an occasional artillery piece, and though its air strength in the Manchurian sanctuary (UN planes were forbidden to attack beyond the Yalu) was growing, it did not venture far from home base. There was no contest whatever for control of the air above the battlefield. The UN had it all alone.

Otherwise, at this stage, and for the first time, the forces were approximately equal. Intelligence estimated that about 400,000 Communist troops, formed in six Chinese armies, faced the Eighth Army, along with the remnants of three North Korean corps. Ridgway commanded about 365,000 men, including the ROK divisions, which were under his control for fighting operations. By now,

BCOF PHOTO FROM UNITED NATIONS

Troops of the Royal Australian Regiment give covering fire to one of their sections pinned down in front of Communist positions.

Bagpipes accompany British troops as they march toward the lines near Suchon.

UNITED NATIONS (FROM BRITISH ARMY)

there were units from Great Britain, Australia, Canada, New Zealand, India, South Africa, France, Greece, the Netherlands, the Philippines, Thailand, Turkey, Belgium, Sweden, and Ethiopia. The average contingent was a reinforced rifle battalion. Most of these small allied combat groups were attached to the U.S. divisions, which made them well over strength. This filling out of the Army, combined with Ridgway's infectious confidence, made the big difference. Operational management became efficient. Forces came to regard themselves as something far superior to an emergency improvisation. "We're good! We're good!" That cry was raised after a successful action. These were permanent gains.

Change of Command

IT WAS a blessing that the Eighth Army found itself when it did, for the next shock did not come from the enemy.

From the beginning, there had been recurrent trouble between President Truman and his great soldier commanding in the Far East, General MacArthur. The detail is unimportant. Most of it was due to the issuing of public statements by the general which the President felt were either injurious to the UN cause or not properly the general's business.

There came a last straw. The UN allies had come to an agreement on their ultimate objectives. Before these objectives were stated aloud to the Communist enemy, an information copy was sent to Tokyo for comment. It was not handled by General MacArthur according to instructions, and there was a resulting embarrassment to the United States in its relations with its fighting partners.

U.S. ARMY PHOTOGRAPH

Lieutenant General Matthew B. Ridgway.

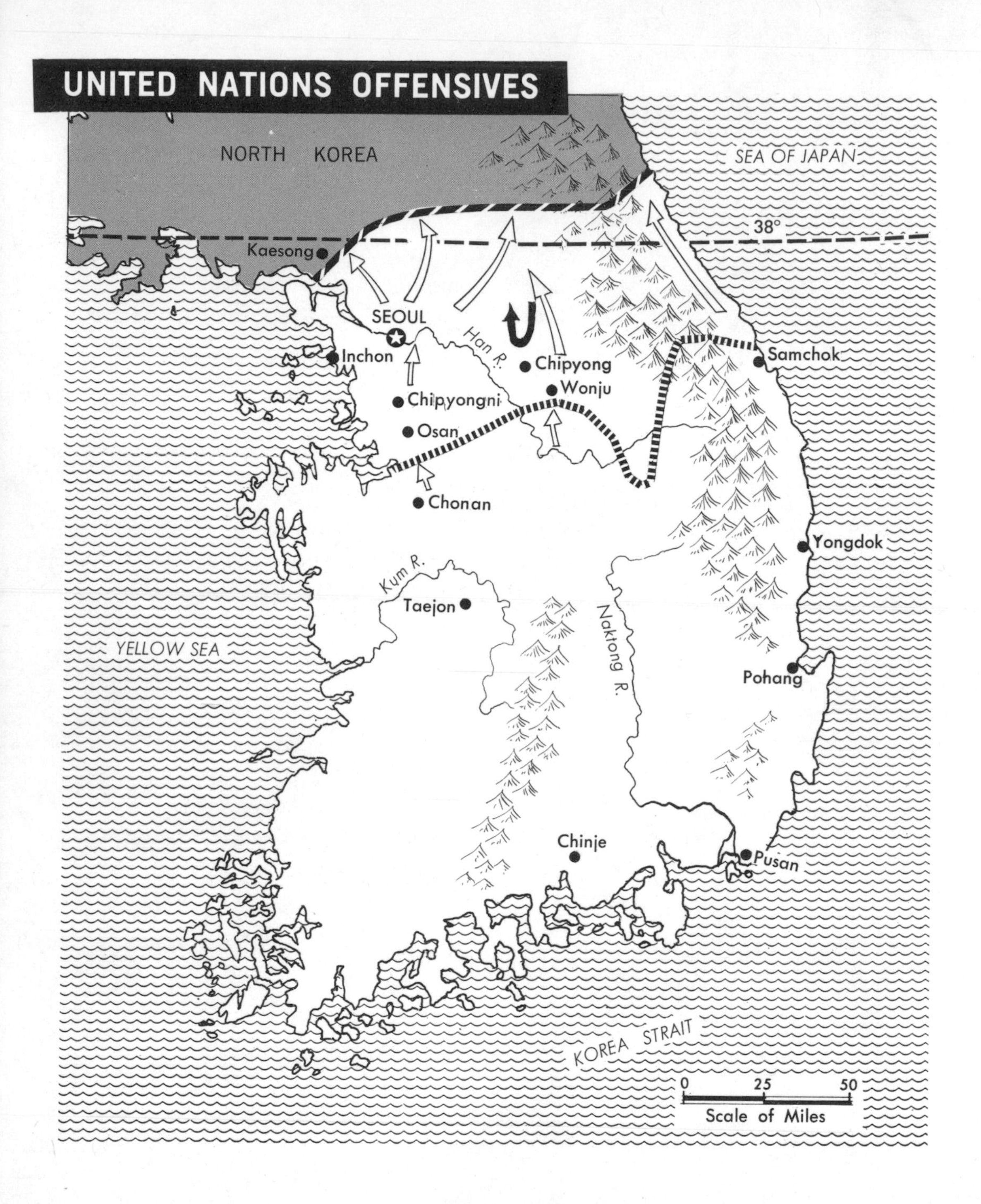
UNITED NATIONS OFFENSIVES
NORTH KOREA
SEA OF JAPAN
38°
Kaesong
SEOUL
Han R.
Inchon
Chipyong
Wonju
Chipyongni
Osan
Samchok
Chonan
Yongdok
Kum R.
Taejon
Naktong R.
YELLOW SEA
Pohang
Chinje
Pusan
KOREA STRAIT
0
25
50
Scale of Miles

The full story of the incident has never been made public. Enough to say that when the President responded by relieving the general of all his commands, the public and press tumult was not quieted by a prolonged Congressional investigation. To millions of Americans who idolized MacArthur, it was unthinkable that he could ever be wrong.

Army Secretary Frank Pace was visiting Ridgway in Korea when he got the word that MacArthur was to move out and Ridgway was to take over. It was Pace's duty to tell both men of the President's decision. He broke the news to Ridgway, then asked: "Now do we congratulate one another or shoot ourselves?"

When Ridgway took command in Tokyo, Lieutenant General James A. (Big Jim) Van Fleet succeeded him as leader of the Eighth Army. This army was already, technically and spiritually, a solid force and remained so. The severe shortages of materiel and technically trained military specialists, which had afflicted all 1950 operations, were now things of the past. There remained one weak spot, however; the ROK Army had no field artillery and too few other heavy weapons. Van Fleet set about immediately to repair this deficiency.

Quickly, the army demonstrated its superior power to its new boss. On April 22, 1951, just eight days after the change of command, the Communists launched their supreme effort of the Korean War, a main offensive over an eighty-mile front, with 200,000 soldiers in the opening attack, and twice that number committed before the five-day battle was over.

The first Communist blow was delivered through the Kwandok mountains of central Korea. By the next day the Chinese were in motion across the whole peninsula. In the center they shattered

UNATIONS

A UN machine gunner waits for the Chinese to attack.

and dispersed the ROK 6th Division, which left a twelve-mile gap in the UN front. Elsewhere, when the onslaught began, the Eighth Army stood firm. Then as the pressure rose higher, the Chinese numbers proved unbeatable in some sectors. North of Seoul, they drove a wedge between the ROK 1st Division and the British 29th Brigade. The three U.S. divisions off the flanks of the Chinese entry retired by slow stages, fighting as they moved.

After cutting the Seoul-Kaesong highway on April 26, the Chinese threw their main weight directly at the capital. Van Fleet decided to stand on Seoul and defend the line of the Han as it runs to meet the sea northwest of the city. Tanks and heavy artillery were emplaced in the very heart of the city. The infantry divisions re-formed on a line four to eight miles north of it, and there they stopped the Chinese.

The UN line had been pushed back from ten to thirty-five miles over most of the front, but the Eighth Army had scored its most impressive defensive victory. The Communist army had paid for its meaningless gains with more than 70,000 casualties, while UN losses were less than one-tenth that number. For once, with all chips down, there had been no wavering. For the first time, the Communist army withdrew from the battle zone. Leaders on that side must have realized at last that they could not win a conclusive victory.

Nevertheless, the Communists made one more hard try. On May 15, one Chinese corps, counting 96,000 men, attacked three UN divisions. This drive hit the east coast sector. One ROK division was split and dispersed, creating a gap which compelled the divisions on both sides of it to give ground. Then the attack collapsed amid a slaughter unparalleled in the Korean War. One U.S. division claimed more than 37,000 Communist casualties while losing only 134 men killed. On that part of the front, enemy resistance virtually dissolved.

Eighth Army immediately lunged forward in hot pursuit, the speed of its rebound showing how radically the balance of forces had shifted. It crossed the 38th Parallel in a solid front. By June 2, its line regiments were back holding the same ground from which they had been driven by the Communist offensive of April 22.

There General Van Fleet called a halt. It was a stratagem aimed to feel out the Communist intentions. He proclaimed on radio that his army would continue to "stop the enemy's unwarranted aggression against South Korea and will, when necessary, meet such threats within North Korea."

U.S. infantrymen try to ward off the deaf ening blast of a 75-mm recoilless rifle.

U.S. ARMY PHOTOGRAPH

Decisions at the highest level of policy-making, rather than the field commander's judgment of situation, caused the stop. It has been debated ever since whether that was wise. To the optimists on the staff it seemed that the easing off came just when a wide open opportunity presented itself. But whether Van Fleet's army was by then sufficiently strong to have pressed on to conclusive victory remains questionable. The roads of North Korea were just as difficult as before. And the farther north his army stretched, the more would it become slowed down and weakened by lack of supply.

But General Van Fleet's comments, spoken during a halt, were interpreted everywhere as a suggestion to the Communists that the time had come to talk peace. Very promptly there came an echo from an unexpected quarter.

The Sitting War

BELATEDLY, the Russians were again sitting in UN, and Jacob Malik was their mouthpiece. He got on the radio and said that, yes, indeed, it was timely to talk peace in Korea.

Immediately nearly everyone believed that peace was coming, probably with a rush. Even the United States Joint Chiefs of Staffs said to one another that the fighting likely would be over within six weeks, or the end might come in half that time.

They were not zealous students of Communist methods in war. Leon Trotzky, who negotiated for the Russians at Brest Litovsk in 1918, put it as a principle that what proletarian armies can't win for themselves on the battlefield, their political overlords must try to gain by wearing down the enemy negotiators at the truce table. If necessary, they would haggle for years. The Chinese leader, Mao Tse-tung, had written that this idea was a pearl beyond price. But even American generals paid little attention to his thoughts.

So, that summer, there were great expectations. These were soon blighted. But in consequence of these peace feelers, coupled with the mandate to the Eighth Army command not to mock them by taking advantage of the temporary defeat of the Communist army, the whole character of the warfare was dramatically transformed.

The war of movement ended. Neither side again launched a full-scale offensive or risked major forces in a bid for total victory. Thus restricted, the ground fighting by the armies had almost no influence on events, and the patrolling of the sea-lanes by the Navy, like the Air Force bombing raids into North Korea, shaped more and more into a routine pattern.

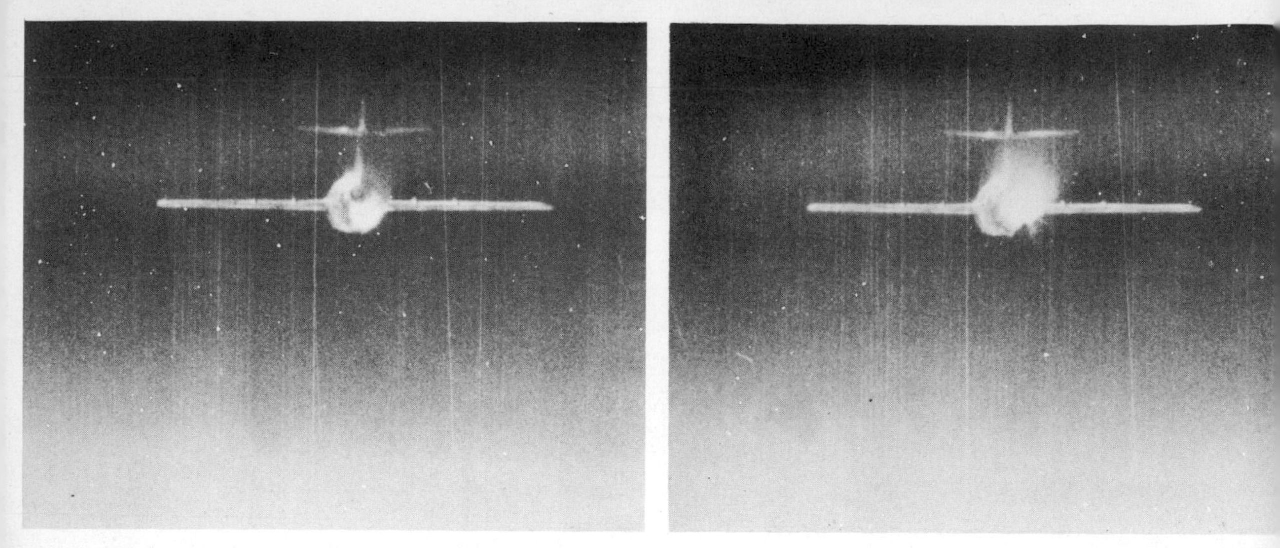

Gun camera strip showing Russian MIG-15 after being

Earlier in the air warfare, there had been several novel developments. For example, on November 1, 1950, an Air Force plane encountered a Communist-manned jet for the first time. Then eight days later a MIG-15 was shot down by an F-80, the first jet-against-jet duel in history. The buildup of a massive Manchuria-based Chinese air force, largely jet-powered, soon followed. When the first Chinese offensive deprived the American Air Force of the advanced bases at Kimpo and Suwon, the Chinese gained temporary air superiority over northwest Korea, and for two months the MIG-15's patrolled rather freely between the Yalu and Chongchon rivers. Long-range F-84E aircraft escorted B-29 missions into this zone. On January 23, thirty-three American fighters engaged twenty-five Chinese fighters near the Yalu and shot down three of them. This was the first great jet battle in any war, and the strong showing by the Chinese surprised everyone. Thereafter, the B-29's were withheld until the UN recaptured Kimpo and Suwon.

The Chinese well understood that their field armies were badly handicapped by the lack of direct air support. But they, too, were

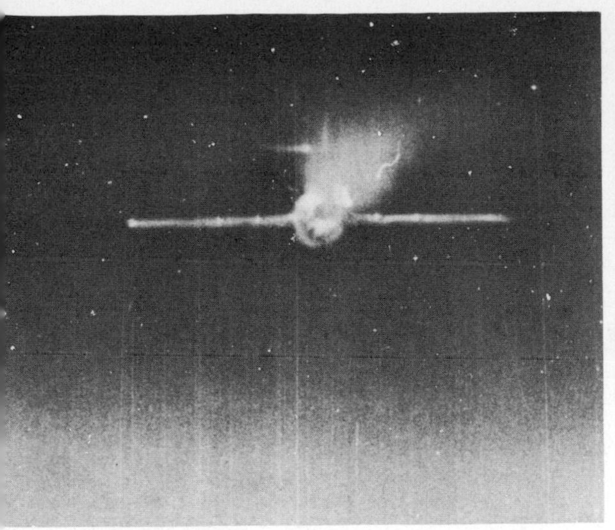
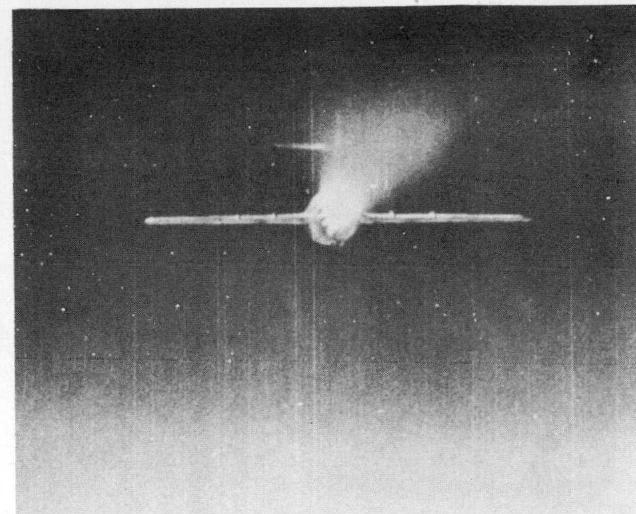

fired on by USAF planes. U.S. AIR FORCE PHOTO

under political restrictions. Planes based on Manchuria were forbidden to engage against UN positions. Russia probably imposed that condition when supplying the Red Chinese with MIG's. Accordingly, in early 1951, the Chinese sent technicians and work crews into North Korea to rehabilitate the wrecked airfields. UN reconnaissance soon showed that many of the airfields were again serviceable. So throughout April, the B-29's went after these fields again, wrecking twelve of them and destroying several score planes on the ground. From there on, the Communists made no further attempt to restore the North Korean bases until after the fighting ceased, and during the rest of 1951 air-against-air action was restricted to a zone nicknamed "MIG Alley," next to the Yalu River.

Warfare between the armies was hardly less strait-jacketed. Local attacks were mounted by both sides to keep troops from going stale and to demonstrate a readiness for resumption of unlimited fighting. These exercises took a heavy toll of life without really helping either side. Both the Communists and the UN built their power higher, the former heavily increasing troop strength,

Two GI's peer through bunker shield at enemy territory.

U.S. ARMY PHOTOGRAPH

the latter augmenting its weapons and adding more artillery and tank units.

The opposing armies dug deeper into their shell-cratered ridges, patrolled against each other by night, killed with artillery and mortar fire around the clock, and occasionally committed regiments or more to a local attack. But while the term, "tactical stalemate," was used to describe this standoff situation, it was a misnomer, for the actual balance between forces was never put to a decisive test. The lines of battle became fixed, first by the UN decision to seek a truce, then by agreement on a temporary demarcation line, and last, by the subordinating of military initiative to the truce negotiations.

The month-long fight for Heartbreak Ridge, in September, 1951, was the first such local battle in the two years of position warfare. Most of the small actions which followed took their names from a single ridge, such as Triangle Hill, Arrowhead, Finger Ridge, Old Baldy, Bunker Hill, Whitehorse, Reno, Vegas, and Pork Chop Hill. Soldiers or news correspondents coined the names, according to the shape of the object on an operations map or some fancied resemblance to a terrain feature back home.

Both Communist and UN defensive lines ran from coast to coast, with strong points and trenches holding to the upper ridge crests. The usual object in pressing a limited attack for one ridge or another was either to straighten the line or gain superior observation.

Even before the demarcation line was agreed upon, both armies entrenched solidly. Thereafter they confronted one another from within two heavily armed, strongly barricaded, and thickly insulated defensive zones. The ridgetops fairly bristled with rock-piled parapets and log-walled bunkers. Every small knob in no-man's-land was also an armored outpost.

Korean porters carry supplies up a hill to UN troops stationed at the top.

SLA MARSHALL

Yet the Eighth Army's front, by comparison, was not thickly fortified. The entrenched main line was formidable; half a mile or less in front of it on lower ground was the paralleling outpost line, each position covered by barbwire all around, with heavily sandbagged works covering the crest. At each one, a platoon or company — depending on the size of the hill — was prepared to fight in isolation. Supplies were run up to the outposts during daylight hours when the enemy artillery usually slept. This was all that the Eighth Army's front possessed of "depth," except that an occasional ridge to rearward was entrenched for use as a blocking position in case the main line broke.

Behind the most forward firing positions held by the Communists, when at last their system was fully developed, the ridges were entrenched to an average depth of fourteen miles. The Communist troops could have fallen back on successive prepared positions for all that distance. The trenches were a maze that presented few profitable targets to the UN air and artillery at any time. The Chinese were so expert with camouflage that there were no easily identifiable gun positions, command posts, or communications centers. Few signs of human life and activity were to be observed either aloft or from the ridgelines where UN soldiers kept watch. The UN bombers could batter down sections of the Chinese trench system whenever they wished, but no real advantage came of it. The surface trenches were manned only by a few widely scattered outposts and sentinels. The Communist garrisons lived under the protection of the ridge mass. Tunnels were run into the ridges from the rear. They led to underground chambers large enough to house a company or battalion. Air bombing and artillery shelling of the ridgetops had no effect on these subterranean shelters, for they were designed to minimize the effects of atomic strikes. The UN had no such invulnerable fortifications.

U.S. ARMY PHOTOGRAPH

U.S. infantry division climbs up a trail to its objective.

From out of these two elaborately engineered and overly protective defensive belts, the opposing armies sparred weakly with one another through the last two years of war. Artillery dueling built steadily upward until in frequency and volume it exceeded the exchanges of World War II. Patrolling and ambushing were of nightly occurrence. Periodically, small fights would develop over possession of a hill or outpost. But that was about all, though both sides were incomparably stronger than they had been in actual battle.

Within three months after the first rumor that truce was possible in Korea, General Van Fleet estimated that the Communist army had expanded to 850,000 men. In that same period, the Communists received their first large shipments of Russian-made artillery and antiaircraft guns. But until just before the fighting ceased in July, 1953, when the Communist army split the front where it was held by two ROK divisions, neither side mounted a main offensive and attempted to break through.

AP WIREPHOTO

Fortified UN position on Korea's western front.

The Bomber War

How did North Korea manage to keep going when the large UN bomber formations could strike against it at will? It is a good question.

Before the first year of war ended, UN bombing attacks had reduced North Korea's industry to rubble. Thereafter the large factories stayed down. Gradually, some production was resumed in hundreds of small plants not identifiable as military targets because they were located in schools, churches, and ordinary houses.

After the Chinese entered the war, the main task of the bomber command was the smashing of troop and supply movements between Manchuria and the battle zone. Operational reports from that period contain such odd entries as "attacked and destroyed military caravan, 17 wagons, 31 ponies, and 16 camels." During the two years of relatively stabilized operations around the 38th Parallel, the heavy bombers were turned against rail lines, bridges, main crossroads, goods trains, and anything that looked like a military depot. But the enemy forces proved to be highly elusive and their communications lines did not prove to be highly vulnerable to this form of attack.

Begun August 18, 1951, and continued until winter by the bomber command, UN "Operation Strangle" was planned to paralyze the Communist rear by destroying junctions, bridges, and all other sensitive points. It was reasoned that if the Communist army were to be deprived of fighting supply, its leaders would have to make peace quickly.

But it was not that simple. Reconnaissance repeatedly revealed that all main bridges were down and the broken rail and highway

U.S. AIR FORCE PHOTO

The Fifth Air Force's 452nd Light Bomb Wing scores a hit on a marshaling yard on the main rail line leading south from Wonsan.

lines were apparently out of use. By night, however, the Communists would bring a retractable bridge out of concealment and traffic would resume full flow. Along railways, dumps of ballast, loose rails, and ties were spaced one-quarter mile apart with a standby crew in walking distance. Convoys and troop columns took to the road by day only when weather prohibited air operations. After the front became stabilized, the enemy rear could hold to these protective measures with no real danger to battle forces.

One of the lasting controversies to arise out of the Korean War has to do with General MacArthur's request that the bombers be permitted to hit Manchuria and the refusal by government to approve. Many claim that the decision denied MacArthur a main chance for victory. The disappointing results of air bombardment against the Communist army in North Korea, after the Chinese came in, should be helpful in weighing the merits of this claim. When the Chinese were so extraordinarily clever at concealing things south of the Yalu, it would seem unlikely that they were wide open to attack in their own country.

On June 23, 1952, the UN bomber command, unopposed, struck

North Korea's hydroelectric power generating plants around Suiho on the Yalu River. The blow was said to have leveled 90 per cent of North Korea's power facility while depriving northeast China of 23 per cent of its power requirement. But the damage resulted in no measurable decline of Communist fighting strength.

These were typical UN air operations, testifying to the complexity of the problems and the intensity of the frustrations. On July 10, 1952, the Far East Air Force published a paper outlining a new strategy. First attention would be given to command of the air; the second objective would be to hit war targets in North Korea; last, Air Force would try to reduce the threat by the Communist armies. This was simple recognition that, due to the changing circumstances of the war, the Eighth Army front required less direct support from the bomber command. But the resulting pattern of air operations was not radically different.

U.S. Air Force grew big during the Korean War, and much of the growth became permanent. Starting with 48 wings and 411,277 people, it increased in two years to 95 wings and 1,061,000 people. Twenty-two of the 27 Air National Guard wings and all 25 wings of the organized air reserve were called to active duty, but remained, for the most part, in the United States. It was characteristic of the war that millions of men were called up but only a small fraction faced fire in Korea.

The Air Force dropped 450,000 tons of bombs and fired 183,000,000 rounds of heavy machine-gun ammunition in Korea. Its fighting aircraft downed 839 enemy MIG's while losing but 53 of their own numbers in engaging them. Overall, the command lost 1,000 aircraft of all types, 110 in air-to-air engagement, 677 to ground fires, and 213 from other causes.

Toward the Truce

WITH THE VOLUNTARY halting of the UN offensive beyond the 38th Parallel in June, 1951, battlefield operations by both sides quickly became secondary to maneuverings at the truce table, and were so treated in the world press.

The truce teams met and argued, first at Kaesong, then at Panmunjom. These conversations went on for two years, broken only occasionally as one team or another withdrew. As a result, activity on the fighting front was restrained almost exactly to the zone where the armies stood when the talks began.

The prolonged wait was due to Communist stalling. Since these tactics were not anticipated and because they proved bitterly disappointing to the United States, the sequence of events by which America was drawn in should be stated exactly.

When General Van Fleet halted his Army, UN Secretary General Lie urged both sides to discuss an end to the fighting. Then quoting Lie, the Voice of America asked the Russian UN delegation to "say the one word the whole world is waiting for." Right afterward, Malik, speaking for Russia, proposed on radio that the two sides get together. On June 28, the Peiping radio spoke in favor of the idea. Next day, President Truman directed General Ridgway to get in touch with the Communist high command and talk truce. The two delegations had their first meeting on July 10, with the Americans truly expecting swift agreement.

The pact was finally signed two years, two weeks, and three days later. The first year of war had cost American forces about 80,000 casualties. During the two years of truce talks, 56,000 more Amer-

American prisoners of war listen to a Communist denunciation of the United States.

AP WIREPHOTO

icans were killed or wounded. It was an expensive lesson in how Communists play politics with human misery.

At first the talks bogged down over Communist insistence that all foreign forces must be withdrawn from Korea before a truce was signed. That was unacceptable to the Americans, because the Chinese Communists could do an about-face and return. Three months later, that item was at last excluded. The conference then agreed on an agenda:

1. Fixing a military demarcation line.
2. Agreement on the conditions of a cease-fire and enforcement of truce terms.
3. Arrangements on the exchange of prisoners.
4. Recommendations to the governments concerned.

AP WIREPHOTO

North Korean General Nam Il and Major General Lee Sang Jo.

When the two teams discussed the first item, they ran straight into another deadlock. There followed quickly a series of suspensions, with each side accusing the other of provocative incidents aimed to sabotage the truce talks. On October 25, the Communists at last withdrew their demand that the truce line should be at the 38th Parallel and yielded to the UN demand that the boundary should be where the armies stood when finally a truce was signed. That agreement practically guaranteed that the fighting would go on.

On December 3 came the next important break. The Communists agreed that no more foreign troops should be brought into Korea and that neutral inspection teams should be admitted to North Korea to verify that the agreement was kept.

On December 11, with hope rising for a truce by Christmas, a conference subcommittee met on the problem of prisoner exchange. Argument over this issue kept the war going another nineteen months, collapsed the negotiations, and led to the loss in combat of another 140,000 UN troops. The crux of the argument was the refusal by the UN delegation forcibly to repatriate 50,000 prisoners who did not wish to return to Communism.

There were 132,000 prisoners in the UN compounds. When the lists were exchanged, the Communists accounted for only 11,559 allied prisoners. The UN delegation reacted violently. The Communist radio had repeatedly claimed that they had taken more than 65,000 prisoners. The mystery of these discrepancies was never solved; the failure of the Communists to explain them built up tension at the conference table.

On January 2, 1952, UN members of the subcommittee on prisoner exchange stated their position in a six-point plan, the critical sentence of which was: "All prisoners not electing repatriation shall be released from prisoner status and shall be paroled." The American government had approved this position, feeling that it would give them a great propaganda advantage. The Communists scorned the idea, and cited Article 118 of the 1949 Geneva Convention which provides that: "Prisoners of war shall be released and repatriated without delay after the cessation of hostilities." Actually, armies rarely abide by this rule when they are victorious; on the other hand, Communists ignore the Geneva Convention except when they can get some advantage from it.

Finally the question was put aside temporarily, and by February 17, 1952, the conference reached agreement on Item No. 4. Indirectly, the Communists passed along the word that they might not fight the six-point plan, provided the number of their people asking asylum of the UN side was not too large. Immediately, the UN army command quietly began polling all prisoners to find out how many wanted to return to Communism. This survey exploded in a series of riots at the largest prisoner-of-war camp on Koje Island, but by the end of the screening the command knew that only 70,000 prisoners wanted repatriation. Two-thirds of the Chinese

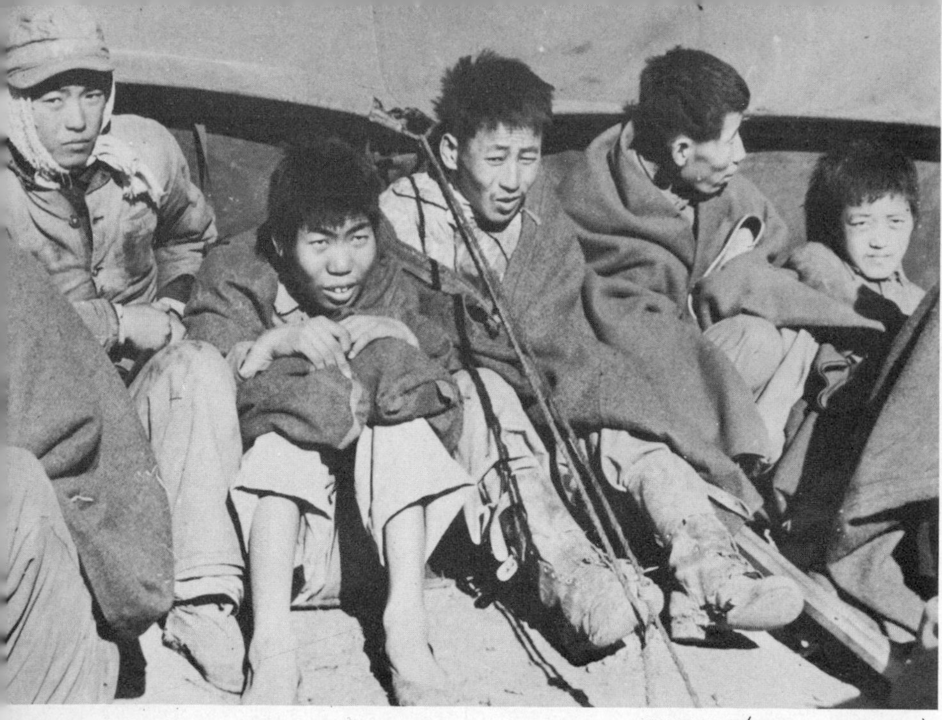

Chinese Communist soldiers captured by UN forces on a Korean fighting front.

UNATIONS (FROM U.S. ARMY)

"volunteers" and about half of the North Korean prisoners said they would not voluntarily return. The response was more embarrassing than gratifying, but with its national honor staked on the position it had earlier taken, the United States could not compromise.

On April 28, 1952, Admiral C. Turner Joy, the chief UN negotiator, announced with finality that, abiding by the principle of voluntary repatriation, the command was prepared to exchange about 70,000 prisoners of war for the approximately 12,000 the Communists admitted holding. Four days later the Communists said no. Truce negotiations stopped. There was no further progress for one year. In May, General Mark W. Clark took over the Far East Command, replacing General Ridgway. A little later, General Maxwell D. Taylor took over the Eighth Army. General Ridgway had to go to Europe to replace General Eisenhower who was about to return home to campaign for the presidency. General Van Fleet

U.S. ARMY PHOTOGRAPH

Two American and four Australian soldiers reach U.S. Medical Clearing Station after being released from captivity in North Korea.

was retired because of his age. Just before election, General Eisenhower pledged that, if he became president, he would go to Korea to see what could be done about stopping the war.

No promising sign of change, however, came of President Eisenhower's visit to Korea. The stalled war droned on another three months with no hopeful interruption. On February 22, 1953, General Clark renewed a long-standing offer to exchange sick and otherwise incapacitated prisoners with the Communists. The bid was routine, and General Clark expected nothing to come of it. But on March 28, to the surprise of the world, the Communist command accepted the offer unconditionally. Its message closed with the expressed hope that the limited exchange would lead to "smooth settlement of the entire question of prisoners of war."

In what was called "Operation Little Switch," staged in late April and centered at Panmunjom, 6,670 sick and disabled Communists were traded for 684 allied prisoners. The returned men were exhaustively interviewed by newsmen who flocked to Korea by the hundreds. So sensational was this story that the correspondents wholly ignored a fierce battle then raging between Americans and Chinese only fifty-six miles from the reception center.

During the exchange, General Clark noted a marked change in the attitude of the enemy negotiators. They had become suddenly reasonable. He said confidentially to a friend: "They act eager; I'm sure now that we will get a truce." Over the Peiping radio, Foreign Minister Chou En-lai was quoted as saying that the two Communist governments were prepared to "take steps to eliminate the difference" between the two camps. That not only signaled that the enemy had weakened on the voluntary repatriation issue; it acknowledged they had miscalculated in believing the Americans would be less tenacious at negotiating, and the Communists would win by patient waiting.

On July 10, 1953, two years from the hour when truce talks were begun, the delegations reconvened at Panmunjom, this time to work in earnest. Agreement became final, and the documents were signed at 10 A.M. on July 27. Twelve hours later the firing ceased.

The final prisoner exchange which soon followed was called "Operation Big Switch." Its course was plagued throughout by bitter argument over screening methods employed in separating voluntary repatriates from those who chose asylum. There were other difficulties. A few Americans – twenty-one of them – at first chose to stay with their Chinese captors, which shocked all their countrymen. Worse still, the American public became unduly upset by the revelation that some U.S. prisoners had behaved shamefully in prison camp. Some had helped the Communists; others had acted brutally toward their comrades. The impact of these

AP WIREPHOTO

The truce is signed.

disclosures far outlasted recollection of how tens of thousands of our fighting men had performed valorously on many now-forgotten battlefields.

As a result, in 1955, a national commission was appointed to go into the story and give judgment. Its findings rebuke those who overemphasize the sordid and discount the admirable. The report points out that the great majority of Americans behaved creditably both on the field of battle and under prison-camp oppression and torture. There were some who could not uphold the high standard. Most of these men were characterless because their childhood was spent in a destructive environment. Societies, like individuals, are never perfect. But they may only become better when the strong have compassion for the weak. Than this, no lesson from the Korean War more deserves underscoring.

The price for this and other lessons came high. The war cost our side 447,697 dead, most of them lost by South Korea, 25,550 lives being the cost to the United States. The toll of wounded on the UN side was 543,893; and again, most of the victims were Koreans, though 103,492 Americans received wounds that qualified them for the Purple Heart Medal.

For America, it was a mighty effort. U.S. contributions in men and supplies literally carried along the UN cause. The United States put into the war seven army divisions, one marine division, army and corps headquarters, logistical and support forces, one tactical air force, one air combat cargo command, two medium bombardment wings, the U.S. Seventh Fleet, and the military sea transport service. Many of the combat units provided by America's allies were armed and outfitted from American stores.

By the end of the war, the UN army in Korea was a modernized force of approximately twenty-eight divisions, plus corps artillery, tanks, and all supporting forces. Within the U.S. Eighth Army, apart from the seven U.S. divisions, there was one division from the British Commonwealth. From ten other allied nations had come the attached battalions, or other smaller contingents. Five nations had supplied medical assistance to the UN command, and forty-eight had offered economic help. The greater part of the growth had occurred within the ROK Army, which was attached to the Eighth Army, but not part of it. The United States had supplied the guns and equipment, as well as the trainers, which made

UNATIONS

A United Nations military cemetery near Pusan.

that growth possible, besides guiding the organization of a modern military school system patterned after its own.

The war itself never ended. In theory, it is going on today. There is only an armistice in Korea, not a formal peace, for no treaty in final settlement was ever signed. The two sides merely stacked their arms, having grown weary of the struggle. Until a more congenial world atmosphere is forthcoming, making possible dependable negotiations between mainland China and the United States, there may never be anything better than an armed truce.

The opposing armies still stand guard along the truce line, with a neutral zone between them. Some years ago the North Korean Army was reconstituted and the Chinese withdrew to Manchuria. The Eighth Army maintains watch along the line where the fighting ended. There are two U.S. divisions (1st Cavalry and 7th Infantry) in this army. Occasionally, the mixed armistice commission meets and haggles over some minor point.

South Korea and the United States are now bound together in a mutual defense treaty. Should there occur another aggression out of the north, America would be automatically at war. This knowledge, more than the presence of the Eighth Army, is the great restraint. It is not a satisfactory situation but we must live with it.

Index

MARSHALL, S. L. A.
The military history
of the Korean War

DATE DUE			
MAY 9			
MAR 4			
GAYLORD M-2			PRINTED IN U.S.A.